HEALING
SPIRITUAL ABUSE
&
RELIGIOUS ADDICTION

Healing Spiritual Abuse & Religious Addiction

Matthew Linn, S.J.
Sheila Fabricant Linn
Dennis Linn

Illustrations by Francisco Miranda

PAULIST PRESS
New York/Mahwah, N.J.

IMPRIMI POTEST:
Bert Thelen, S.J.
Provincial, Wisconsin Province of the Society of Jesus
September 9, 1993

Library of Congress Cataloging-in-Publication Data

Linn, Matthew.
    Healing spiritual abuse & religious addiction / Matthew Linn,
Sheila Fabricant Linn, Dennis Linn.
        p.   cm.
    Includes bibliographical references.
    ISBN 0-8091-3488-8 (pbk.)
    1. Spiritual life—Catholic Church.   2. Religious addiction—
Christianity.   3. Catholic Church—Membership.   4. Linn, Matthew.
5. Linn, Sheila Fabricant.   6. Linn, Dennis.   I. Linn, Sheila
Fabricant.   II. Linn, Dennis.   III. Title.   IV. Title: Healing
spiritual abuse and religious addiction.
BX2350.2.L495   1994
253.5—dc20   94-13408
                                                                  CIP

Published by Paulist Press
977 Macarthur Boulevard
Mahwah, N.J. 07430

Printed and bound in the United States of America

Contents

ACKNOWLEDGEMENTS

We wish to thank the following people for their gift of time and care in reading the manuscript for this book and offering suggestions: Millie Dosh & Dr. Terry, Barbara & Dr. Morton Kelsey, Rev. Jack McGinnis, Pat & Pia Mellody, Sr. Mary Sharon Riley, R.C., Barbara Shlemon Ryan & Timothy Ryan, Dr. Douglas Schoeninger, Rev. Robert Sears, S.J., Rev. Paul Smith, Dr. Len Sperry, Rev. William Thompson, S.J. and Dr. Diana Villegas.

All scripture quotations are from the *Revised New American Bible*, unless another version is indicated.

DEDICATION

This book is dedicated to

Rev. Leo Thomas, O.P.
Rev. Flora Wuellner
and The Society of Jesus

in gratitude for teaching us to trust our experience and to
find the presence of God in all things.

Introduction

Several years ago, Ann asked a friend of ours to pray with her husband. Ann complained that her husband never went to church or to the prayer meeting. All he wanted to do was sit in front of the television and watch football games.

Ann wanted God to make her husband more spiritual. For Ann, "spiritual" meant that he would pray and attend church as much as she did. Ann believed Jesus prayed all the time, and so did she. As Ann had become increasingly absorbed in prayer and church attendance, her husband had become less and less interested in these things. His wife wasn't any fun and he figured Jesus wasn't either.

Sensing that the one who really needed healing was Ann rather than her husband, our friend asked if he could pray with her. As our friend prayed with Ann, he could see that she felt deeply moved by what was happening. Suddenly Ann burst out laughing. She said that she had seen Jesus come into her house, go through the kitchen door and into the living room, which was a mess. Ann felt embarrassed, because she would have cleaned up the house if she had known Jesus was coming. But the mess didn't seem to bother Jesus.

Jesus asked Ann where her husband was. Ann answered that he was in the basement watching televi-

*sion. Jesus went down the stairs into the basement.
When he didn't reappear for a while, Ann went down-
stairs and found Jesus sitting on the couch next to her
husband, watching the football game.*

*Ann understood that Jesus wanted her to do the
same thing. Jesus wanted her to stop overusing prayer
and churchgoing, and start enjoying life with her
husband.* [1]

For us, this is a story about how sometimes religion makes
people healthy and sometimes it makes them sick. What makes
the difference?

We have learned about addictions from the Twelve-Step
recovery movement. The addictive process was the focus of our
book *Belonging: Bonds of Healing & Recovery.* Our field is spirituality and we have become aware that the dynamics of addiction
(using a substance or process to escape from our own reality,
especially painful feelings) can affect our spiritual life, so that
religion itself becomes our drug of choice. In Ann's case, we
don't know why she substituted constant prayer and churchgoing
for a real relationship with her husband. If it was to escape from
painful feelings in her marriage or in other areas of her life, then
we might guess that Ann had a religious addiction. Her efforts to
use religion to control others, e.g., by trying to impose her religious practices upon her husband, support our guess.

Many people besides ourselves have become aware of this
misuse of religion, and several books have appeared recently that
describe religious addiction very well. Sensitized by these books
and by our own growing awareness, and armed with the label
"religious addict," at times we find ourselves tempted to judgmen-
tally categorize those who use religion to control others. This
happens especially if their efforts have ever been directed against
ourselves. However, we've learned that all addictive behavior
comes from deep pain and contains a cry for healing. If that cry is

not heard and answered, then recovery is superficial and the addict may simply substitute one addiction for another. For example, the alcoholic who has stopped drinking, but whose emotional pain remains untouched, may well begin smoking or overeating. In fact, those who have renounced addictive behavior that looks "bad" (such as sexual promiscuity or drug abuse), but who are not fully healed emotionally, are especially likely to substitute religious addiction because it looks "good."

Although we might wish that those who misuse religion would simply get with it and be converted to our own "progressive" attitudes, we know it's not that simple. At least it hasn't been that simple for us. Dennis and Matt's recovery from religious addiction is an ongoing process, and all three of us are slowly recovering from spiritual abuse. We have not always been as ready as Ann to let go of distorted forms of religiosity.

This book contains what we have learned about religious addiction and spiritual abuse. The first two chapters describe religious addiction and spiritual abuse, and the healing that can come from spiritual reparenting. Because addiction and abuse are rooted in shame, Chapters 3 through 6 explore the shame-based patterns we learn in childhood that can make us vulnerable to religious addiction and spiritual abuse, and how these patterns can be healed through recalling positive and negative memories. Chapter 7 expands this healing to include the abuse and shame suffered by our ancestors (still expressed through conflicts in many of the most troubled places in the world today). Chapter 8 discusses how scripture has often been used to reinforce religious addiction and spiritual abuse. Finally, Chapter 9 is about healthy religion, in which we, like Ann, are free to do what Jesus would do.

This book is not only for those in recovery from religious addiction and spiritual abuse. We are writing for anyone who, like ourselves, is searching for a more life-giving relationship with God and with a healthy faith community.

1

Spiritual Abuse & Spiritual Reparenting

In Alice Walker's *The Color Purple*, Celie and Shug talk about God. Celie has just described God as the one she was taught to believe in by white people. Shug replies:

Ain't no way to read the bible and not think God white, she say. Then she sigh. When I found out I thought God was white, and a man, I lost interest. . . .

Here's the thing, say Shug. The thing I believe. God is inside you and inside everybody else. You come into the world with God. But only them that search for it inside find it. And sometimes it just manifest itself even if you not looking, or don't know what you looking for. . . .

My first step from the old white man was trees. Then air. Then birds. Then other people. But one day when I was sitting quiet and feeling like a motherless child, which I was, it come to me: that feeling of being part of everything, not separate at all. I knew that if I cut a tree, my arm would bleed. And I laughed and I cried and I run all around the house. I knew just what it was.[1]

Shug and Celie's journey from God as an abusive white man to God found within oneself and the entire universe is a journey of recovery from spiritual abuse and religious addiction. I (Sheila) want to introduce the ideas of spiritual abuse and religious addiction by sharing with you how my own spiritual journey has led me to name them and to form a certain understanding of what they are.

I come from a Jewish family. My grandparents were very observant Jews, my parents less so. My mother was seriously ill all of her life, with what we think was a form of minimal brain damage. Because of her illness, she could not create a secure home. As a result, I was not well bonded to my nuclear family. I did receive nurturing from my grandparents when I was a small child, until they moved away when I was eight.

I also received from my grandparents a *feel* for Judaism, especially in its reverence and respect for all of creation and for the human person. That reverence and respect is expressed in the love of learning that is so strong in Judaism. In my Jewish community, I found a commitment to search for the truth and never to be afraid of what we discovered. Judaism as I know it is profoundly incarnational. I grew up believing that God is present in all things.

This belief came not only from the environment of Judaism, but also from my own experience. I frequently escaped from my parents' home by walking in the forest that bordered our neighborhood. I would look at leaves and stones and blades of grass, noticing how beautiful they were. Often I felt caught by a particular leaf or blade of grass. I would sit down and look at it for a very long time, overwhelmed by its goodness. At those times I sensed a presence behind it, as if the leaf or blade of grass were a window to something larger than itself. That something was personal, and it was loving. Sometimes there would be a shift, and it seemed as if that something was looking back at me, noticing *my* goodness and reminding me that my real self was loved.

As a child, I was aware that my mother was not free to be her real self. This began a question within me that I carried into adulthood. My question was, "Why are some people free to be their real selves, and others are locked up inside?" I wanted to know how the locked up ones could be set free. It wasn't an entirely selfless question. Except for those moments in the forest and occasional visits with my grandparents, I felt locked up inside. My parents had not given me permission to trust my own reality or to be my real self.

When I went to college, I thought the best place to look for the answer to my question was in psychology. However, throughout my freshman year I became increasingly troubled by the psychology courses I was taking. I noticed that we spoke only about things that could be diagrammed or measured. We could not use words that described things that could not be quantified, words like "truth" or "love." I knew something was missing.

At the end of the year, I was attending the final meeting of my Abnormal Psychology class. The professor used an overhead projector and colored markers to illustrate his lecture. He drew a red arrow and said, "That is the aggressive drive." Then he drew a blue arrow and said, "That is the sexual drive." He drew a green blotch and said, "That is the introjection of Mother." He drew a brown blotch and said, "That is the introjection of Father." He went on in this way for a while, and finally he drew two black brackets around the whole thing and said, "That is a human being." I said to myself, "No, it's not!" I knew then what I had been missing: the mysterious depth dimension of human beings that cannot be diagrammed or measured.

I was an undergraduate at Duke University, which has an excellent religion department. My roommate, Judith, wanted to be a minister, and she was a religion major. Judith sensed what I needed, and she encouraged me to take a course in the religion department. I signed up for a theology course, on Paul Tillich, Martin Buber and Michael Polanyi. One of the first classes was on Polanyi, who wasn't really a theologian at all but rather a physicist.

Polanyi wrote about how we acquire knowledge. He said it required a loving commitment to truth and a leap of faith. There was what I had been missing: words (e.g., truth, love, faith) that had depth and mystery. I decided right then to become a religion major. I found out that the religion department had many courses in psychology and religion. I took all of them. I was still studying psychology, but now through a different lens, the lens of spirituality.

Because I was in the religion department, I was around many of the most committed Christians at Duke, including those who wanted to go on into ministry. I began to sense a certain presence in those students that I couldn't identify. I knew that I knew it, but I didn't know its name. It was personal and it was loving. It reminded me of those experiences of nature I'd had in the forest as a child. By the time I was ready to graduate, I knew I was on the right track of my question and I wanted to continue. It occurred to me that if I went to divinity school, I could study pastoral psychology. I applied to the Master's of Divinity program at the Graduate Theological Union in Berkeley, still identifying myself as a Jewish person.

At the GTU I met two of the most significant people in my life. Both were teachers there. Flora was a Congregational minister who also taught spirituality. Leo was a Dominican priest who taught pastoral counseling. Flora and Leo loved me in a way that I had not felt loved since I was a small child with my grandparents. They made a home for me inside themselves. They trusted me and they encouraged me to ask questions. They each had that same presence I had sensed in the natural world as a child and in my classmates at Duke. Flora and Leo had it especially thick. "What is it?" I kept asking myself.

Then one day I was sitting out on the back stairs of my seminary, reading the Bible. A thought came to me very quietly: "Its name is Jesus." I felt still inside, with the relaxed feeling that comes when I've remembered a name that I had temporarily forgotten. I was recalling something I had always known. I also knew this was the answer to my question; I knew that somehow the loving presence whose name is Jesus could set people free. I said to myself, "This is what Christians believe. I must be a Christian now." I spent the next year deciding in what church I belonged.

If there was a single moment when I decided to become a Roman Catholic, it was in a theology class. The professor quoted St. Thomas Aquinas as saying that if we pursue reason all the way to the end of where it leads us, in an honest search for truth, then reason will never contradict faith. I felt as if I had come home to the spiritual environment of my grandparents. For me, St. Thomas' words meant that creation, including my own heart and mind, could be trusted and that honest questions were not to be feared. Such questions were themselves a way to God.

Wonderful Surprises

I began to notice that good theology always had a surprise. There was a certain quality to the Christian vision, in which things ultimately turned out to be better than we could ever have planned. It came to me that a sign of grace or of the Spirit, in Christian theology anyway, is this certain quality of a wonderful surprise. I noticed this in the outer world, and also in the inner world.

It was around this time that I got involved in Catholic Charismatic Renewal through what appeared to be a healthy prayer group. I learned about inner healing prayer. As I experienced Jesus loving me in the midst of early hurts, he showed me that I could trust myself. Sometimes the feelings and reactions that I had most disliked in myself turned out to be my best friends, expressions of a profound inner wisdom about who I was and what I needed. There were wonderful surprises inside me, too.

Also at this time I was taking several courses in theology and science at the Jesuit seminary. As I studied the evolutionary process, I saw that evolution was always doing something that contained a wonderful surprise. Evolution had the same quality I had sensed in good theology and within myself. As Brian Swimme puts it, "The universe is addicted to surprise."[2] I knew I needed a spirituality that would help my heart and mind grow as big as the evolving universe.

This whole process of psychospiritual growth was possible because I was in an atmosphere of love. I was bonded to two people who loved me; I felt that I belonged to Flora and to Leo. I'm sure it was significant that they were an older man and an older woman—I had spiritual parents. My bonds with them nourished my bond with God.

The religious educator Martin Lang speaks of how the foundation for religious faith is not religious education itself, but strong family bonds. A child who is tightly bonded to its parents has the psychological foundation for religious faith, whereas a loosely bonded child may know doctrines but has little psychological capacity to trust God.[3] Once, after I had become a Christian, I was visiting a Jewish synagogue. The rabbi was preparing for the service, and his young daughter was helping him. I felt deeply moved by the obvious closeness between them, and I thought, "If I had experienced such close bonding with my Jewish parents, I wonder if I would ever have become a Christian."

I didn't experience close bonding with my Jewish parents, and I needed Leo and Flora. They were healthy Christian parents, in that they wanted me to think what I think and feel what I feel. Leo gave me instruction in Catholicism. The best thing he did was to express great respect for Judaism. He told me that God would love me every bit as much if I never became a Christian. Leo was protecting my spiritual freedom. Because he did so, my decision to join the Church was never contaminated by shame or fear.

Flora, too, protected my spiritual freedom. She gave me books on every kind of spirituality: books on healing prayer and books on reincarnation, books by Catholic saints and books by psychics. She didn't believe in all those things, but she wanted me to think for myself.

In my whole environment at that time, I was free to think, to explore, to trust my questions, to learn about my real self—to think what I thought, to feel what I felt, to believe what I believed, and to be surprised. I was experiencing the first principle of Christian theology, which is that God is always infinitely bigger than our ideas of him or her. As the Jesuit priest Ed Dowling said to Bill Wilson (co-founder of Alcoholics Anonymous), "If you can name it, it's not God."[4]

Those seminary years were my formative experience of Christianity. Ever since, I have measured Christian groups, leaders, churches, etc., by the same criteria: is this a place where each person's spiritual freedom is protected? In the years since then, the answer has often enough been "No" that now I have a different question than the one with which I started. The question I started with was, "How can locked up people be set free?" I decided the answer was Jesus. Today my question is, "Why does Christianity set some people free but leave other people more locked up than ever before?" By "locked up," I mean more rigid, more distant from their real selves, less able to think what they think, feel what they feel and want what they want. Since I'm still recovering from a nuclear family where I was discouraged from trusting my own reality, it's frightening for me to think that members of my Christian family might be discouraged from trusting our own reality. Why does this happen?

Religious Addiction & Spiritual Abuse

I've begun to find an answer through our work with addictions and recovery. I've learned that an addiction is any substance or process we use to escape from and get control over a painful reality in our lives, especially painful feelings. We use something outside to escape from and control something we're afraid of inside. As Anne Wilson Schaef says, the purpose of an addiction is to put us *out of touch* with ourselves.[5]

It has become clear to me that we can use religion or religious things in exactly the same way as drugs or alcohol, to escape from what is real within. The underlying addiction is to control.

Religious addiction attempts to control painful inner reality through a rigid religious belief system.[6]

For example, perhaps I feel unsure of myself and as if I don't belong anywhere. I cannot face my feelings of shame, loneliness and fear. Thus, I compulsively read the Bible or rigidly adhere to all the teachings of the Church, looking for absolute answers and a sense of belonging. Whenever that pain tries to come up, I get out my Bible or I go to Mass or I quote the pope. Or, perhaps I have been deeply hurt and I am very angry, maybe even filled with primitive rage if the hurt was an early one. I have been taught to feel ashamed of such feelings and I am terrified of them. I believe that "good Christians" forgive, and I remind myself of Jesus on the cross. I tell myself that every time I don't forgive I am putting another nail in his hands. Whenever that anger and rage try to come up, I use Jesus on the cross to get them under control. Since denied feelings such as shame, anger and rage do not really go away but instead only build up within, the next time such feelings come up I may become even more rigid in my use of religion to get them under control.

Because my need to control inner reality through a rigid belief system is so desperate, I insist that everyone else believe in the same way as myself. Anyone who doesn't threatens my system of controlling my inner pain. Thus I have created a world where there are no surprises, inside or outside, because I'm too afraid of them. I am now *off* the track of evolution, and off the track of my own human process of growth. If I have children, or if I am a religious leader, I may spiritually abuse those who are looking up to me. By spiritual abuse, I mean that I will deny their spiritual freedom by telling them there is only one way to God, *my* way— because anything else is too threatening to me.[7]

My favorite story about St. Ignatius (the founder of the Jesuit order) is that he would fire spiritual directors who tried to impose their way to God on novices. St. Ignatius understood that it is abusive to try to control another person's spiritual journey.[8] Unlike St. Ignatius, spiritually abusive parents or religious leaders use children or followers to meet their own needs for control and self-esteem, rather than nurturing the spiritual development of those who look up to them.

I don't want to blame such people for what I am calling spiritual abuse and religious addiction. What better drug of choice than a perfect, all-powerful, all-knowing God out there who controls everything and everybody? Well-meaning people are set up for this in a culture that does not teach us how to deal with painful feelings, and in a church that has often taught us that the truth is in the Bible, in the pope, in the ministers or priests, in the sacraments . . . everywhere but inside ourselves. Religion is often taught as a system of control, of rules, of rituals, of ideals: of shoulds. It's very easy to use all this to squelch the process of life, all the while thinking we're being good Christians. Shame-based people are particularly vulnerable to this, having been raised in a way that taught them not to trust themselves.[a]

---

a) The addictive potential of religion comes not only from its capacity to "hook" shame-based people, but also from its use of ritual. All religions, especially those which emphasize the sacraments, recognize the human need for ritual. Ritual creates an altered state of consciousness, in which we are more able to experience the transcendent. However, this altered state also makes us vulnerable to outside manipulation and control. Thus, spiritual abusers may consciously or unconsciously use ritual to create an altered state in victims, in order to gain control over them. The result is ritual abuse. Ritual abuse takes place not only in satanic cults but also in mainline churches; the difference is the severity of the abuse and the severity of the symptoms in the victim. Victims of satanic ritual abuse are often so terrorized that they split into subpersonalities which are separated by barriers of amnesia. Victims of religious ritual abuse are rarely so terrorized, but they may have symptoms as extreme as dissociative disorders and post-traumatic stress disorder. Perhaps ritual abuse can be thought of on a continuum, ranging from very severe to less severe abuse. Thus satanic ritual abuse would be very severe abuse, an extremely rigid Catholic or fundamentalist school where children are intimidated into religious practices might exemplify less severe abuse, and a liturgy or religious service celebrated by a

Our intention is not to say that the Bible or the hierarchy of the Church have no truth to offer us. The Bible and the hierarchy are carriers of the Christian tradition, and that tradition is as essential to our Christian life as the food we eat is to our physical life. None of us can create on our own the wisdom accumulated over thousands of years of Judaeo-Christian history. However, we can't relate to the carriers of this tradition properly if we are out of touch with or trying to escape from our real self. Then religious things can become substitutes for a real self, in the same way as can food, alcohol, drugs, sex, or a co-dependent relationship with a person. When we substitute the carriers of religious tradition for a real self, we give up our own voice and therefore our capacity for dialogue. It seems to us that a healthy relationship with tradition is a conversation in which the dialogue enables both the individual and the tradition to change and grow.

I chose to become a Catholic. Although I respect those who leave, I would make that same choice again today because I love Catholicism. I believe it is my responsibility to relate to the Church in a healthy way and to avoid misusing good things like the papacy, the Bible, religious vows, the sacraments, etc. I misuse these good things when I substitute them for a real self or when I substitute them for God. These things are helps in my journey to God, but they are not the fullness of God. As Karl Rahner said, "God is always greater than what we know of him, and greater than the things which he himself has willed."[10] If I pretend otherwise I am involved in idolatry. If I substitute religious things for a real self, I am involved in religious addiction.

Jesus never meant us to use him or any other religious thing as an escape from the truth of our lives. Two friends of ours put it this way: Christianity was not meant first of all to teach us doc-

---

religious addict might exemplify still less severe abuse. A ritual celebrated by a religious addict will almost always be ritually abusive, because it is most likely an attempt to use ritual to control the spiritual journey of others.[9]

trines, but rather how to process life.[11] Although not everyone may define the role of Christianity in exactly this way, I find that doctrines and religious practices are helpful when they support my capacity to authentically process life. I believe that Jesus wants to walk with us as we do this. The more we authentically process life and the more the truth of ourselves unfolds, the more we reveal God who dwells in the core of our being.

Thus, I have come to understand the difference between healthy spirituality and religious addiction as follows: I believe that healthy spirituality is whatever helps us to process life, whatever helps us to be with the truth of who we are. I believe that religious addiction is whatever we use as a substitute for processing life, as an escape from the truth of who we are.[12]

Spiritual Reparenting

Religious addiction is a ministry issue for me, but first it's a personal issue. One of the ways my parents could not parent me was spiritually. I don't mean they failed to give me religious instruction; they sent me to Hebrew school, which provides religious education for Jewish children. But they could not stand behind and encourage my unique spiritual journey.

Thus far we have defined spiritual abuse in terms of what is done, such as trying to control the spiritual journey of another. But just as emotional or physical abuse can include neglect, i.e., what is not done, so can spiritual abuse. My parents did not give me positive models of healthy spirituality, nor did they teach me how to trust my inner self.

In his book *Shame*, Gershen Kaufman says that children need not only to see how parents live, but to be let in on the inner process by which parents arrive at their decisions of how to live.[13] As a child, I needed to know what it is like on the inside of a spiritually healthy adult. In other words, I needed to know how healthy adults process life. Because my parents could not reveal this to me and could not support my spiritual journey, I needed spiritual parents like Flora and Leo.

Like many inadequately parented people, I was susceptible to almost anyone who offered the safety, nurturing and belonging that I needed. I mentioned above that while I was in seminary, I joined what appeared to be a healthy prayer group. This prayer group gradually became unhealthy, as the leadership changed and as the new leaders were exposed to teaching that emphasized authority, submission and the subordination of women. At the prayer meetings we began to hear that we (the members) had the light. The "others" (presumably just about everyone else in the San Francisco Bay Area) were in darkness. The voices of women were now rarely heard at the meetings. We were asked to enter a new covenant agreement with the community, in which we sub-mitted major life decisions to "pastors." The implication was that commitment to the community equalled commitment to God. Eventually, the entire community (several hundred people) was urged to move to the midwest, where we could join forces with another large community in our battle against "the world." There we would be protected from those dangerous people who thought differently from ourselves. I now recognize much of this as the behavior of a cult, but at the time a part of me was very vulnera-ble to the pressure exerted by the community. I struggled with the decision of whether to enter their new covenant agreement and move to the midwest. I desperately wanted to belong, and that is what the community seemed to offer.

I also noticed increasing feelings of shame during the prayer meetings, and a desire to escape. When the leaders spoke, I felt as if someone were pounding on my head. I longed to go outside and sit under a tree, where the evening air seemed so gentle in comparison. There, I felt free to be myself.

Fortunately, I listened to these feelings. Fortunately also, I knew a few people back at the seminary whose healthy spirituality gave me a frame of reference in which to evaluate the prayer group. Besides Flora and Leo, I knew a Jesuit priest named Jim. I shared with Jim how disturbed I felt during the teachings at the prayer meetings, as if someone were pounding on my head. Jim told me that these feelings were clues to where God was leading me. He pulled out his copy of *The Spiritual Exercises of St. Ignatius*, and turned to the section on "Rules for Discernment of Spirits." He read me the following passage:

> In souls that are progressing to greater perfection, the action of the good angel is delicate, gentle, delightful. It may be compared to a drop of water penetrating a sponge.
>
> The action of the evil spirit upon such souls is violent, noisy and disturbing. It may be compared to a drop of water falling upon a stone. [14]

I was immediately aware that my sense of being pounded on the head during the prayer meetings was like the thud of water falling on a stone. Outside under the tree, the gentle air felt like a drop of water penetrating a sponge. Jim told me to trust my awareness. In that meeting with him, Jim provided healthy spiritual parenting. He encouraged me to feel what I felt and think what I thought. He (and St. Ignatius) also let me in on the way in which spiritually healthy adults process life and arrive at decisions (e.g., by attending to inner movements). Jim's healthy spiritual parenting of me protected me from the unhealthy parenting at the prayer group. I decided not to commit myself to the community's new covenant and not to move with them to the midwest. Today, knowing the subsequent history of that community as I do, I believe it would have been disastrous for me to have remained with them.

It would have been disastrous for me to remain partly because this particular community had become unhealthy, and also because I had outgrown the kind of structure found in many such tightly organized communities. When I first joined the community, I was at a stage of development in which I needed a lot of external structure for my faith. By the time I left, however, I had grown to where I no longer needed that kind of structure. Just as emotional abuse includes expecting a two-year-old child to behave like a ten-year-old, or keeping a ten-year-old as dependent as a two-year-old, so spiritual abuse includes pushing people to a stage of faith development for which they are not yet ready, or trying to keep them at a stage that they have outgrown.[b]

Religious addiction hurts and frightens me because many times, as with the prayer group described above, I have opened myself to people who I thought would protect my spiritual freedom. Instead, they have told me that there was only one way to find God—their way. Looking back, I think I joined the Church because I was looking for the bonding I missed as a child and for a healthy family where I could learn to trust my own reality. Sometimes I've found that. Sometimes I have felt betrayed, as if I now have two dysfunctional families rather than the one I started with.

I think many of us have had these experiences. I was fortunate to escape from that prayer group. Others, with the same needs for spiritual parenting as myself, have not been so fortunate

---

b) Just as human beings pass through stages of emotional development (identified by Erik Erikson) and stages of cognitive development (identified by Jean Piaget), we also pass through stages of faith development (identified by James Fowler). Not all human beings reach the highest levels of development, but a healthy environment is one that encourages us to keep growing.

A behavior that in one person is a symptom of religious addiction, in another person may be normal for a particular stage of faith development. For example, reliance on external religious authority is a common symptom of religious addiction and is also typical of an early stage of faith development. If reliance upon external authority temporarily helps provide security and structure for continued growth into higher stages, then it seems to us a part of healthy development. However, if reliance upon external authority is a way of compulsively avoiding one's own reality, then it seems to us more likely a sign of religious addiction. A measure of whether a particular religious behavior is healthy and stage-appropriate, or addictive, might be our ability to tolerate and gradually move toward respect for and even dialogue with those who are different.[15]

and have been trapped in spiritually abusive environments. We hope this book can help us to heal such experiences, and to receive the healthy spiritual parenting we needed and deserved.

This book will also encourage us to thank those people whose love for us gave us a glimpse of what healthy spirituality is by helping us find our own unique way of belonging to God. Such people reveal something we first heard from Anthony DeMello: "God loves you at least as much as the person who loves you the most." If anything in this book doesn't sound at least as loving as the person who loves you the most, then it is not God's voice. If you are not sure how God might be inviting you to a healthier spirituality, you can ask, "What would the person who loves me the most say about this?"

PRAYER PROCESS

1. Recall an experience of religion in which others encouraged you to explore, to think what you thought and feel what you felt—a time when God became big, bigger than you ever imagined. Who were with you and what did he or she say or do that gave you such a sense of freedom? How did you feel? Breathe in again the love and freedom you felt in that situation.

2. Recall an experience of religion in which you did not feel free to explore, a time when you were told there was only one way to believe. How did that feel? Who do you wish had been there with you? What do you wish that person had said or done?

3. Notice the difference between how you felt in these two experiences. What does this say to you about what kind of religious environment is healthy for you and what isn't?

4. You may wish to thank God for both experiences, and for how they can guide you in discerning your own way to God.

2

Sexual Abuse & God the Mother

Once upon a time an international meeting was held on an American ship. In rough seas, the ship crashed into a rock. Water gushed in. The American captain, realizing the fast-sinking ship had but one small lifeboat, went on the deck and tried to convince everyone to jump and swim for shore. He returned in frustration and told the American co-captain that no one would jump for they feared drowning. The co-captain said, "Don't worry. I'll take care of it." Five minutes later the co-captain called the captain to the deck. Sure enough, everyone had jumped. As feared, all who jumped had drowned. So the captain asked the co-captain, "How did you get them to jump?" The co-captain said, "It was easy. I told the British that it was proper to jump, the French that it was stylish, the Irish to offer it up, and the Germans that it was commanded. Finally, I told the Italians it was forbidden to jump, and they jumped too." Then it occurred to the American captains that they did not have to use the lifeboat either. After all, they were insured. They jumped . . . and drowned.

Need for Primary Relationships to Reparent Us

I (Dennis) know of few families who tried to unconditionally love their children as much as my family did. However, regardless of how good a family or culture we come from, all of us carry wounds that can make us jump at the wrong times. This is because none of our families are God; thus none of our families are perfect. Last year, during a couples' retreat, I drew up a list of eighteen ways I was wounded as a child. (For example, growing up in the age of Sputnik, I was encouraged in the "hard" sciences, while art, dance and music were devalued.) What surprised me was that Sheila has extraordinary gifts in fifteen of those eighteen areas, and she has given me exactly what I needed to fill in childhood wounds. I've become a believer in marriage therapist Harville Hendrix's theory that the intensity of romantic love comes from our bodies' heartfelt joy over having finally found the person who can heal us of our wounds. Healing can happen because we pick for a spouse someone who is like our parents (to help us recall our childhood wounds), yet also different (to provide us with what we didn't get). Thus one of the many healthy relationships that a husband and wife can have is that of reparenting one another. [1]

Reparenting, filling in what we missed in our childhood, happens not just in the spousal relationship but in many relationships in our lives. In the previous chapter Sheila spoke of how Flora and John reparented her. Much of the growth in my life has also come because of the people like Flora and John who have reparented me.

Just as allowing Sheila to reparent me adds joyful intensity to our love, so too with God. The more I allow God to reparent me, the more intense my love relationship with God. For instance, I was raised in an Irish-German family. The Irish, afraid things would get even worse, "offered up" everything from stomach aches to Uncle Ted's alcoholism. When I was twenty-five years old, friends introduced me to a God who could heal everything from stomach aches to relationships. This God reparented me by taking me back one by one to the hurtful memories underneath the chronic stomach aches that I had offered up, and gradually healed me. My life changed so much that I have written eleven books to share my enthusiasm about this healing God.

I needed reparenting by God not only on the Irish side but also on the German side. Although I don't want to stereotype all Germans, I inherited German self-righteousness. After experiencing so much other healing from God, I prayed long and hard to be healed of my German self-righteousness, but little changed. Finally I realized that the reason I didn't change was that my God was German. My self-righteous German God sat on his (I had an all-male God at the time) judgment throne and saw all the mistakes and errors in everyone. If he didn't like what he saw, he distanced himself and even sent some to hell.

We not only become like our parents whom we adore, but also like the God we adore. In our last three books I have shared how healing of my German self-righteousness happened when I changed my image of God. It's not that I no longer see the mistakes and errors in others. Rather, I usually see the same thing in myself so I no longer feel distant from that person. This change occurred in me because, instead of a judgmental German God, I now have a God who reparents me by loving me in shameful memories that I had buried and forgotten because I feared God's harsh judgment.

As my needs changed, I discovered yet another way that God wants to reparent me. It is the main way that God has reparented me during the past five years. You may need to be reparented in an entirely different way than I do. As I share my journey, you might wish to ask yourself: Is there any way that I want God to reparent me now?

How God Reparents Me Now

The best way to describe how God reparents me now is by sharing a dream I had nearly five years ago. In the dream, two hands skillfully massaged a wounded body. I had no idea whose hands these were. I only knew that each time I tried to take over and massage that same body, all the bones began breaking. The more I failed, the more I longed to know whose hands these were that continued so skillfully to massage and mend the body. Finally, I saw a man who looked like a doctor boarding an airplane. I asked, "Were you the one giving the massage?" He looked puzzled.

Then I heard a voice say, "Honey, you are looking in the wrong direction." I turned around and followed those two hands upward. I found myself looking into the face of God, with her gracefully flowing black hair. She smiled at me and said reassuringly, "I am the God of the dream, the God of the unconscious. I am going to heal you."

This dream occurred during the first day of a thirty-day retreat. During that thirty-day retreat I could hardly wait to go to sleep because each night I would receive another dream. I had planned to make the thirty-day retreat according to the *Spiritual Exercises* of St. Ignatius. The *Exercises* guide retreatants through a sequence of spiritual movements designed to bring healing and interior freedom. After eleven days of dreams, I asked my director if I should stop working so much with my dreams and instead begin formally making the *Exercises*. He handed me a stack of cards containing images representing various desires and feelings. He asked me to pick out only those cards that represented something that I had experienced during the previous eleven days. I matched various cards with various dreams and then organized the cards on the floor, beginning with my first dream. My director then showed me how I was receiving in each night's dream the healing that the *Exercises* would have led me to pray for the following day. He sent me back to bed so that my body-massaging God, "the God of the dream and the unconscious," could continue to heal me. I would like to share some of this healing with you, and why I so desperately needed this body-massaging God (whom I now call "God-My-Mother") to reparent me.

My Childhood and My Need for Reparenting

Several months ago, I sat down and within five minutes wrote the ten riddles that I memorized over thirty years ago, on May 24, 1962.

1. I have two coins worth thirty cents in value, one is not a nickle, what are they?
2. There are five apples on the table and I take two apples, how many do I have?
3. What is two divided by half?
4. How do you keep fish from smelling?
5. When is coffee like the soil?
6. How is the letter "t" like an island?
7. An apple and a banana were on top of the Empire State Building. The apple jumped off. Why didn't the banana?
8. I have a house with all four sides facing south, a bear walks by, what color is the bear?
9. I go to bed at eight o'clock at night and set my alarm clock for nine o'clock the next morning. How many hours sleep did I get?
10. What goes up to a house and doesn't go in?

Answers: 1. Quarter and nickle. 2. Two. 3. Four. 4. Cut off their heads. 5. When ground. 6. It's in the middle of water. 7. It was yellow. 8. White. 9. One hour. 10. Sidewalk.

May 24, 1962 was the date of my senior prom. As a high school student, I was a very scrupulous person and disliked myself. Because of that I had never dated. I agreed to attend the senior prom only because of peer pressure. I made sure that two other classmates would triple date with me. I was hoping these four other people, my date, and my ten memorized jokes would fill any lulls in the conversation. I was wrong. I never dated again.

Religious Addiction and the Death of My Sexuality

Why was I so scrupulous and why didn't I ever date? In the culture in which I grew up, the heroes were priests, religious sisters, and the Blessed Mother. All were celibate and wore flowing religious garb that made them look bodiless. They were so asexual that I remember how shocked I was in seventh grade when I discovered that priests went to the bathroom. Shortly afterward, I began wondering if it was possible that religious sisters did too. I took on many of the "bodiless" attitudes I perceived in my pastors and religious teachers. They taught endless rules about the "do's" and "don'ts" of sexuality. Any infringement was a serious sin and especially offensive to God, who (it seemed to me) saw sexuality as bad. I must be bad too, I thought, because I didn't see how I could ever live up to all those rules.

One summer, for example, our family went on a two-week trip. On the first day we stopped at a gas station that had a calendar showing Marilyn Monroe with most of her body hanging out of a skimpy swim suit. After staring at her seductive pose, I became frightened that I had committed a mortal sin. I spent the rest of the two weeks thinking I was in mortal sin and afraid we would have a car accident in which I would die and my soul would go immediately to hell.

Death and hell constantly filled my thoughts. Death seemed

like a daily possibility since my brother John died suddenly at age two. Besides, we lived less than one block from the district air raid siren. Every Tuesday its shrill shriek reminded us of the Russian nuclear threat and sent us scrambling under our school desks. Many thought that the Russian nuclear threat, which meant almost certain destruction of the world, coincided with the secret Fatima message. This message, given by the Blessed Mother at Fatima, was secret because only each pope who opened it knew what it said.

Each time I heard about a pope opening the Fatima letter, I feared the world would end that very day. On such days, I got up early so that I could go immediately to confession. This made me feel somewhat safe for the rest of the day. I say "somewhat" safe, for in religion class we often heard a story about some boy who for years lived a sinless life. Then one day that boy (why weren't those stories ever about girls?) committed a deadly mortal sin. Maybe he passionately kissed his girl friend or enjoyed a porno-graphic picture.[a] As luck would have it, the boy died the same day. The story always ended with God weeping because, of course, God had no other choice but to send the boy into the fires of hell.

By waking up early and going to confession, I could take care of what I thought was a major mortal sin like the one I committed by staring at the calendar in the gas station. My soul would once again become spotless-white, like the sinless children in those

---

a) This may sound extreme, but at the time most Roman Catholic teach-ing about sexuality reflected the 1612 declaration of Claudius Aquaviva (the General of the Society of Jesus). He declared that with regards to sexuality there was no parvity of matter. In other words, any deviation from the rules was a mortal sin. Until Vatican II, the Church felt constrained by this authoritarian declaration, and never attempted to debate or discuss it. Sexuality was the only area of moral theology where we always assumed that everything was grave matter.[2]

stories. But what would happen if later that day, I experienced an "impure thought" as I again dwelt on the picture of Marilyn Monroe? Unfortunately, our parish had weekday confessions only in the morning. Thus I was grateful that every night my family not only prayed the rosary for the conversion of Russia but also prayed the Act of Contrition together.

A "perfect" Act of Contrition, our Irish pastor Fr. Daly assured us, was the only prayer that could forgive mortal sins outside of confession. The Act of Contrition went like this:

> O my God, I am heartily sorry for having offended thee. I detest all my sins because I dread the loss of heaven and the pains of hell. But most of all, because they have offended thee, my God, who art all good and deserving of all my love . . .

The Act of Contrition was "perfect," Fr. Daly explained, only if my detesting "of all my sins" came as a result of having "offended thee, my God, who art all good and deserving of all my love" and not as a result of dreading "the loss of heaven and the pains of hell." In other words, you had to be concerned about loving God and not about saving your own skin. I had tested what the fires of hell felt like by seeing how long I could stand the pain of keeping my finger over a lit match. Because I often prayed the Act of Contrition thinking about that burned finger and thus to literally "save my own skin," my contrition seldom measured up to Fr. Daly's standard of perfection. Thus I often lay awake at night worrying that I would die suddenly, just as those other children with only one sin. What a relief to wake up the next morning and discover I wasn't in hell yet. On such mornings, I gladly headed over again to Fr. Daly's confessional. As I developed normal adolescent sexual feelings, my fear and shame increased. Thus I buried my feelings under even more religious practices.

In short, I became a religious addict going to confession, daily Mass, visiting the Blessed Sacrament and multiplying every religious practice possible in order to save my soul. Several times a year, I'd tally up all my religious practices and present them as a "spiritual bouquet" gift to some lucky person. A spiritual bouquet might include five or six thousand ejaculations. That's because in a single day I could repeat perhaps two to three hundred times (I kept track on my rosary beads) short prayers called "ejaculations," which earned "indulgences." If you were going to hell anyway, indulgences didn't help. But if you were lucky enough to merit only the punishment of purgatory, indulgences were credit stored against the punishment your sins merited. "Jesus, Mary, Joseph" was my favorite prayer because each time I said it, I merited seven years' indulgence. No other three-word ejaculatory prayer gave such a high reward. The fact that I didn't even know "ejaculation" was also a sexual word reveals how much religious addiction had distanced me from my own body.

Because I wanted so desperately to save my soul, I entered the Jesuit novitiate three months after my senior prom. We were taught that religious life was "a higher calling." Of all the religious orders, the Jesuits had the longest training and I knew my blackened soul needed all the help it could get. I did get some facts straightened out in the novitiate, like the day I learned that the only way you could conceive a child was through intercourse. In high school we were all tested on so many rules as to how far you could go in kissing, necking and petting that I figured maybe these somehow brought on pregnancy too.

I would not trade my years of Jesuit life for anything. Like my parents, my Jesuit family taught me what unconditional love meant. I knew that both families had and would lay down their lives for me. However, before 1966 and the changes of Vatican II, Jesuit life was not as healthy as it is today. Thus much of what in 1962 the Jesuits may have thought was the most loving thing to do, now they would readily admit was not healthy. For instance, as novices we each received "misery beads" to keep track daily of the number of times we transgressed a rule. Since women were temptations to our celibate vocation, we had a number of rules that discouraged talking to them or even looking at them ("custody of the eyes"). My misery beads got a lot of action, not only because my impure thoughts about the calendar continued, but also because the rules in the novitiate had added a lot more sexual sin possibilities to my list. To fight against temptations of the flesh, most of us whipped our bodies several times each week before lights out. The sound of the whip heard up and down the hallways was just another reminder to me of how bad my body was and how much I needed the discipline of religious life to save my soul. Two years after entering the novitiate, with this perverted view of sexuality and my body, I took permanent vows as a Jesuit.

Twenty-five years later, I had the dream about the hands skillfully massaging a body that I now know was mine. God, with her long flowing black hair, knew that healing for me had to begin by helping me return to my whipped body. Just how God-My-Mother would help me return to my body is best explained by the second dream I had about her.

Second Dream: Returning to My Body

I dreamed that I was hurriedly riding my bicycle to the airport. I knew I would be late for my airplane, so I was relieved when I spotted a yellow taxi parked in front of a house. I rang the doorbell, and a woman holding a faceless, blob-like child answered the door. I said, "I need a cab driver to help me catch my plane." The woman responded, "The driver will be right with you," and closed the door. No driver came. So I rang the doorbell again. When the woman opened the door, I asked, "Well, where is the cab driver?" Pointing to the faceless blob in her arms she said, "He is your cab driver."

I knew the dream meant that if I wanted to catch my plane or get where I am going in life, I needed to help that faceless blob (my inner child) grow up. In the following weeks I dialogued inwardly with the woman, letting her tell me my childhood history and how I became a bodiless, faceless blob. I have already shared much of what the woman told me, from the calendar in the gas station to a "perfect" Act of Contrition and finally novitiate misery beads. But there is one more story, from my infancy. To introduce it, I want to share an experience with my sister's baby, David.

One evening when David was four months old, my parents and I were visiting my sister, Mary Ellen. David began crying. As soon as she heard David's cry, Mary Ellen was on her way to David's room to pick him up. My father stopped her and said, "That baby just wants attention. You'll spoil him. Wait until he stops crying. Then go pick him up." What followed was a very long and heated discussion. I remember David's frightened face when Mary Ellen finally picked him up twenty minutes later. One look at David convinced her that she would have to continue disagreeing with my father. She picked David up, held him tightly and apologized for the way she had ignored him.

The woman in the dream shared with me incidents of myself crying as a baby and, like David, not getting picked up. Each time, after I had cried a long time, my face had David's frightened look. I realized that when I stopped crying, I always got picked up. It didn't take me long to figure out that crying wasn't welcome. But to shut off crying, I had to shut off the feelings and needs that caused it. As I did so, the fright on my face faded away, and I became a faceless blob.

That faceless blob reminds me that every culture has blind spots. Many writers have addressed the German blind spot of not picking up a crying baby for fear of spoiling her or him.[3] This view of discipline, even though in my case carried out with the most loving intentions, led me to disconnect from my body.

We now know that some babies who are not picked up literally disconnect by shutting down their bodies and dying of an illness called marasmus. The main way a baby communicates the urgent messages of its body is through crying. Suppose, for instance, that a baby needs to be held. If the baby cries to express this need and someone comes and lovingly holds it, the child thinks: "My needs must be good because they bring me all this care. Therefore the needs I feel in my body must be good, and I am good." On the other hand, if the child's cry is not answered, the child thinks the opposite: "The needs I feel in my body only bring me abandonment. Therefore my body must be bad, and I must be bad." Rather than constantly face intense feelings of abandonment, a baby will shut down its body. Thus, German discipline, which triggered deep feelings of abandonment in me, taught me to shut down my body: not to feel what I feel, think what I think, or trust what I trust.

Shutting down our bodies in this way is the root of addiction. An addiction is the use of any substance or process to escape reality, especially painful feelings. In my case, even as a baby I shut down my body as a way to escape painful feelings of abandonment. An addiction is also our best attempt to belong.[4] Shutting off my body was my best attempt to get what I needed in order to belong (e.g., to get picked up and held). When my body was shut off and therefore unable to communicate troublesome needs, I felt safe. As I grew up, I developed addictions to foster this safe feeling. In my family, religion was one of the easiest ways to get a sense of belonging. I became a religious addict, using ejaculatory prayers and external rituals to keep me from feeling what I felt, thinking what I thought, and trusting what I trusted.

I knew I needed to come back to my body. But just knowing this didn't seem to help me that day as I considered the image of myself in my dream, a bodiless, faceless blob. That's why I felt relief when, in my imagination, the woman who was sharing my story with me stopped talking. She bent over and scooped up my tiny faceless blob and held me tightly. She apologized for how I was treated and began breastfeeding me. As she did so, some of the features gradually returned to my face. Finally, her hands began to massage the rest of the blob. I could feel myself unfolding. My body began to look like that of a normal child. As I felt those hands massage me so skillfully, I knew this woman was God-My-Mother.[5] For many days I returned to her in my imagination and let her continue to breastfeed me and massage me. This healing seemed so primitive and basic that I knew if I simply rested in it, it gradually would transform many of the times in my life when I felt bodiless and faceless, whether or not I consciously remembered all those times.

I began to change. For instance, for several weeks her massaging seemed to make my backbone grow. I began feeling like a tall, rooted tree. For the first time in my life, I even painted pictures of such trees. Usually I climbed one first and rested quietly against a large branch until I could feel its backbone growing along with mine. During those weeks I knew my body was beginning to have "backbone." Finally I was feeling my own feelings, thinking my own thoughts, and trusting myself. As God-My-Mother of both my dreams knew, for me the way out of addiction or other destructive behavior is the journey back into my body.

God-My-Mother and the Reawakening of the Feminine

Another way to speak about the journey back into my body is the journey into my feminine side. An image of how estranged I was from my feminine side is that of the clumsiness of my senior prom. I feared dancing because instead of living in my body, I lived mostly in my mind, graduating in the upper 2% of my class. As I mentioned previously, instead of developing my feminine side through learning dance, music and art, I learned math and science. Although I prayed to both the masculine (God the Father) and the feminine (the Blessed Mother), they weren't equal. Only the masculine Father was God. And so it was with my life: the masculine was God. I was as ill at ease with girls as I was with my feminine side. My senior prom was my first and last date.

I come out of two families. Along with Sheila, these two families are the most significant conduits through which the best things in my life have come to me. I could never thank them enough. Yet, despite all their gifts, these two families both wounded me in a similar way. Before my senior prom I lived in a family where negative emotions as well as the inner affective life in general were looked down on and judged harshly. After my senior prom I lived in a celibate Jesuit family in which there was great wisdom about the interior life, but where this wisdom was often distorted by male clericalism. Both families left me with a masculine skew: I was great at getting things done, thinking for myself, and finding God "out there." I did not sufficiently develop the feminine values of simply being, listening to feelings and body wisdom, and finding God within.

Forming deep friendships with women over the years certainly opened me up to my feminine side. But it was still such a struggle for me, like being in a foreign land. I prayed for healing of the hurts that had put me out of touch with my feminine side, but very little changed. A year after these prayers, however, I experienced profound change. I began to feel at ease with the feminine world. I changed because during that year my image of God changed. This change in my image of God was not only an intellectual shift, but also a deeply felt affective shift.

We not only mimic many of the traits of our families, but we also mimic the traits of our God. My God had been a male celibate. No matter how hard we pray for healing, we generally become only as healthy as the God we adore. When I became comfortable with not only praying to Jesus or God the Father but also to the feminine side of God, God-My-Mother, my "male skew" hurts began to heal.

Erik Erikson's essay, "Womanhood and the Inner Space," broadened my understanding of what I had experienced.[6] Erikson describes the ways the masculine physiologically and psychologically emphasizes outer space, while the feminine focuses on inner space. He suggests that the masculine image of God is more transcendent (a mighty God who is "out there," always inviting us to change and grow). For years, in order to change and grow, I had tried everything from becoming a celibate Jesuit to daily confession and healing prayer. Some things helped me but others didn't. I still needed the feminine side of God.

In contrast to the masculine side, Erikson describes the feminine side of God as more immanent (a God within who is present in whatever we are experiencing). This God communicated from within me through dreams, breastfed me and massaged my body just as it was. With her I could just be. She never told me a word about how I should change or grow. I need to be cared for by both sides of God, just as I needed the unique ways of caring that both my mother and father offered me as I grew up. The airplanes in both of my God-My-Mother dreams were signs that, for right now, she would get me where I needed to go.

God-My-Mother and Healing of Sexual Abuse

I needed God-My-Mother to reparent me, so that I would no longer sexually abuse others in the ways that I was abused. Often when we think of sexual abuse, we think of physical or genital abuse. I have never abused or been abused in that way. Perhaps sexual abuse also happens in many other ways.[b]

---

b) We are not using the word "abuse" in the strict legal sense, where certain extreme behaviors of one person harming another, such as an adult raping a child, have been defined as grounds for criminal prosecution. We are using "abuse" in the broader, popular sense, to mean any situation in which a

With any illness or dysfunctional behavior, until we are honest about all the ways it manifests itself, we are caught in denial and unable to recover. For example, the childhood stories of spiritual abuse that I have shared were considered normal, healthy behavior by many Catholics until Vatican II. Although people had an awareness of obvious spiritual abuse in previous centuries, such as the religious persecution of Jews, they were often unaware of how it was happening to them every day. Once Vatican II gave us a new vision of what is healthy, we moved to a new level of awareness of what is spiritual abuse. Many behaviors that before we considered "normal" we could now recognize as spiritual abuse, name them as that, and thus begin recovering.

Just as greater awareness helps us to recognize and recover from spiritual abuse, so also with sexual abuse. Getting through denial is important to me because for most of my life I did not think I had been sexually abused. At our workshops we often speak about sexual abuse. Because I limited it to physical or genital abuse, Sheila, who had experienced such sexual abuse, always gave the talk. Now both Matt and I know that there is a sense in which we, too, were sexually abused and we can add to Sheila's talk.[c] For instance, for both of us to grow up with an all-male image of God was sexually abusive. So were the teachings and religious practices that made me afraid to date and separated me from my sexuality. The three of us now sometimes speak of sexual abuse in a broader, metaphorical sense, to include any way we are not encouraged to develop and trust both the masculine and feminine sides of our personality and of our image of God.

---

person with more power (e.g., parent, religious leader) hurts a person with less power (e.g., child, follower).

c) In saying that we were sexually abused, we are not saying that anyone intended to sexually abuse us or realized that they were doing so. We are saying

Recently, in revisions of our 1978 book *Healing Life's Hurts*, Matt and I apologized for things we said in that book that we now realize are sexually abusive. First, we apologized for our clericalism idealizing celibacy and the vows. We had spoken of "vocation" as if the word applied to religious alone. Secondly, we apologized for the male skew in our examples, such as pushing people to change rather than encouraging them to be loved where they were. Our male skew had also idealized autonomy and working things out alone with God, and minimized the feminine value of interconnectedness that reminds us to include other human beings (a friend, support group or therapist) in the process. Thirdly, we apologized for our sexist language and examples in referring to people and to God. For instance, we had suggested that the model for healing hurts comes from the story of the prodigal son, in which God the Father throws a party and welcomes us home (Lk 15:11–32). Because we were so into our male skew, we completely skipped over the story immediately above, of the woman who found the lost coin. This story describes how God the Mother also wants to throw a party and welcome us

---

that the effects upon us of growing up in a patriarchal church culture were similar in some ways to the symptoms of a sexual abuse victim. Sheila, who did experience sexual abuse in the literal, physical sense, finds a similarity between what that abuse did to her in the past and what the patriarchal church environment does to her today. In other words we are describing abuse from the side of the wounded victim, and not judging the intentionality of the perpetrator.

Because of our desire to be sensitive to victims, we struggled over whether to use the term "sexual abuse" in this broader sense, to include the religious practices and teachings described in this chapter. On the one hand, we hesitated because we did not want to minimize the horror of physical sexual abuse, which for many people (like Sheila) is far more traumatic than anything we are speaking of here. On the other hand, we want to tell the truth about how severely religious practices and teachings can damage our sexual identity. We also want to honor the voices of many people who have told us, "I am being sexually abused by the institutional church."

home (Lk 15:8–11). Removing sexist language and using this and other scripture stories of God as Mother (Num 11:12, Is 49:15, 63:15, Ps 131:2) would be for us symbols of our desire to stop our ways of sexual abuse and to perceive our inner and outer worlds in a new way.

None of us can grow any faster than our image of God. For instance, none of us can relate to an only male God without stunting the growth of our feminine side. Developmentally, what each person is growing into is the image of God. As Meister Eckhart wrote,

> The seed of God is within us. Now the seed of a pear tree grows into a pear tree; and a hazel seed grows into a hazel tree; a seed of God grows into God.[7]

In other words, each person is a developing face of God (Gal 2:20; Gn 11:26–27). We need to sense a congruence between our own identity and our image of God in order to keep growing. If we don't have both sides of God, we either have to abandon God as God has been presented to us, or we have to abandon our own growth, i.e., we betray our potential to become integrated human beings.[8]

Until Matt and I came to know the feminine side of God (and of other people), our personalities were stuck in many ways in the pre-adolescent stage of male psychosexual development. What happened to Matt and myself has also happened to much of the Church. Churches, too, become like the God they adore. Like ourselves, the Roman Catholic Church has a male clerical skew. Thus it emphasizes the male values of authority, efficiency, law and a transcendent God, to the detriment of feminine values such as mutuality, being, inner body wisdom, and an immanent God.

Although my experience has never included physical sexual abuse, recent insights into the causes of child molestation by clergy help me understand how I became stuck in psychosexual development. "The Report of the Archdiocesan Commission of

Enquiry into the Sexual Abuse of Children by Members of the Clergy," issued in 1990 by the St. John's, Newfoundland Archdiocese, "is without exception the most important statement on celibate/sexual morality issued under church auspices in the past fifty years."[9] The report says that the patriarchal, clerical structure of the Roman Catholic Church creates a climate that significantly contributes to child sexual molestation by priests.[d] Commenting on this report, and based upon his twenty-five years of studying the celibate clerical system, A.W. Richard Sipe of The Johns Hopkins University School of Medicine says,

> . . . it is clear that the institutional Church is in a pre-adolescent stage of psychosexual development. This is a period typically prior to eleven years of age in which boys prefer association with their own sex, girls are avoided and held in disdain, often as a guise for fear of women as well as of their own as-yet unsolidified sexuality. Sex generally is rigidly denied externally while secretly explored. The rigidity extends to strict rules of inclusion and exclusion. Control and avoidance are of primary concern.
>
> This institutional structure, although it surely includes individuals who have matured beyond it, is dominated and

---

d) Because the issue of child sexual molestation by priests is currently such a painful and sensitive one in our church, we want to acknowledge genuine efforts to confront it. The most outstanding is the Newfoundland Report itself, which admits the underlying systemic disorder of patriarchy and clericalism. Although we do not know of any other diocese that has both publicly acknowledged and addressed the underlying issue, we do see recent signs in some dioceses of efforts to respond to the problems of child sexual molestation and other inappropriate sexual behavior. The National Conference of Catholic Bishops recently established a committee to address these problems. The committee's tasks include aiding victims, monitoring offenders so they are not simply transferred to other ministry situations where they are likely to offend again, and improving the selection process for candidates to the priesthood.

entrenched in a level of functioning that cannot face the sexual realities of adolescence, let alone mature male and female equality and sexuality. [10]

As Richard Sipe suggests, a church stuck in the pre-adolescent stage of development is limited in its ability to cope with sexual issues and give sexual guidelines, as I was at the time of my senior prom. Thus many Catholics question the Church's guidelines in sexual matters such as divorce and remarriage, birth control, abortion, homosexuality, mandatory celibacy for priests, women's ordination, and limiting ultimate decision-making to males. Many such people cherish the Church's good values, such as the sacredness in all instances of human life, the intuition that reproduction is a sacred link to God's creativity, and the sacramental value of married love. However, such values are often lost in discussions of sexual issues. One reason this happens may be that the institutional Church interpreting and promoting these values is often stuck in a pre-adolescent stage of psychosexual development. Thus, the main message many people hear is not the Church's good values, but rather an underlying fear of women and sexuality. It is this negative, fearful attitude that many people may be rejecting when they question Church teaching on sexuality. [11]

The more God-My-Mother reparents me, the more I and the entire Church can not only stop sexually abusing others, but even more grow into the image of God that we were meant to be.

HEALING PROCESS

1. Recall a time when you held a child in your arms. Perhaps it was your own child. Perhaps it was a grandchild, a niece, a nephew, or the child of a friend. Recall the love in your heart toward that child, how good and precious it seemed to you, and your desire to protect it and give it every good thing. (If you prefer, recall holding a pet.)

2. Now imagine yourself in the arms of God the Mother. If you cannot imagine God the Mother, rest in the arms of your mother, grandmother, or another woman who has given you God's motherly love. Be aware that she holds you as lovingly as you held that child. She sees you as good and precious. She wants to protect you and give you every good thing.

3. Rest in the arms of God the Mother (or another motherly figure), perhaps recalling the words of Isaiah 49:15,

> "Can a mother forget her infant, or be without tenderness for the child of her womb? Even should she forget you, I will never forget you."

4. Breathe deeply, filling yourself with her love for you.

Introduction to Chapters 3 Through 7: Four Roles That Make Us Vulnerable to Spiritual Abuse and Religious Addiction

In the previous two chapters, we introduced the ideas of spiritual abuse and religious addiction. The following five chapters are intended to help us uncover and heal our learned patterns of handling shame, so that we might be less vulnerable to spiritual abuse and religious addiction.

Many people working in the field of recovery believe that the core emotion in both abuse and addiction is shame. The word "shame" is sometimes used to refer to a healthy awareness of our human limitations (e.g., the ability to admit we don't know an answer that others expect us to know). At other times, and in the sense we use it throughout this book, "shame" means a toxic, debilitating core sense of being unlovable and inferior as a person. [a]

---

a) Shame is distinct from guilt, in that guilt refers to disliking what we have done and shame refers to disliking who we are. A popular way of expressing the distinction is: "Guilt says I made a mistake; shame says I am a mistake." [1]

Addictions, such as religious addiction, are a means of escaping painful feelings, primarily shame.

For example, I (Dennis) as a religious addict would compulsively multiply religious practices such as confession, visits to the Blessed Sacrament, rosaries and ejaculations. These addictive religious practices temporarily helped me feel good about myself by burying my feeling of shame—the gnawing sense that I was no good and deserved hell. In the long run, however, addictions never work because shame, or anything else we bury, will return with even greater force.

My buried feelings of shame and my religious addiction set me up for even more spiritual abuse. Thus, feeling deep down that I was no good and deserved hell, I kept returning to those who spiritually abused me by telling me that I was a sinful person and that, if I wasn't faithful to the religious practices they required, I would indeed go to hell. My hope was that such people, understanding my dire situation, might offer me some other religious practice (such as whipping my body) that might save me. But instead of offering me something that really could save me, both whipping my body and the abusive teachings on hell only demeaned and devalued me further. They filled me with even more shame, which I would again try to bury through even more religious practices.

Only when my image of God changed and I allowed God the Mother to massage the faceless blob that contained my shame, did that shame fully heal as I began growing a backbone, like a tall, rooted tree. As my body developed backbone, I could stand up to my spiritual abusers and stop the cycle of spiritual abuse and religious addiction. The healing of shame frees us from both.

Most of us learned our patterns of handling shame in childhood. How did you handle shame? You might want to try the following exercise. Imagine that you are three years old, and you know that your mother keeps candy up in the cupboard. Imagine your kitchen. Now see yourself moving a chair over to the cupboard, climbing up on it, and spying the candy hidden behind a stack of cups. Reach for the candy and take a piece. Now as you take your hand away, you accidentally knock over a cup. It falls to the floor and shatters into a million pieces. Feel the shame and how your body wants to curl up into a fetal position and disappear. Your mother or father comes and says, "Shame on you . . ." How would you feel and what would you do?

Family therapists have found that children have four major ways of dealing with such shame. These are the four roles that children take in a dysfunctional, shaming family. One child, often the oldest, says to itself, "I will try harder and be more careful next time." This child becomes the *responsible child*, who deals with shame by striving to be good. Another child, often a younger one who can't compete by being good, says to itself, "Who cares? I am bad so I will act bad." This child becomes the *rebel*, who deals with shame by acting out. A third child wants to disappear and run from the shameful scene. This child becomes the *lost child*, who as a shy introvert continues to quietly withdraw or adjust to avoid further shame. A fourth child, often the youngest who was doted over, covers shame by getting positive attention through distracting humor. This child becomes the *distractor*, or extroverted, fun-loving entertainer.[2]

These roles are just four possible ones. They can appear in any child in any combination, regardless of birth order. When there is a gap of more than five years between children, the younger is even more free to choose any role.[3]

It seems to us that some of the groups in Jesus' time were also stuck in these shame-based roles, and therefore vulnerable to spiritual abuse and religious addiction. Thus, in the following section we will compare the four family roles with the responsible Pharisees, rebel Samaritans, lost Essenes and the distractor Sadducees. Although each of these groups at times became spiritually abusive and/or religiously addicted, each group also (like each of the four family roles) had a special gift.

You may find yourself in each of these religious types. As types, they are not likely to be an exact fit, but rather a guide to finding a part of yourself that is both gifted and wounded. You may find you have too much of a particular type's compulsion, or too little of its gift. Ideally, we have something of all four types, since each needs the balance of the others' gifts. The problem with the four family roles is not the roles themselves, but our stuckness in any one. They are meant to be fluid, integrated aspects of a healthy personality, just as the groups in Jesus' time were meant to be fluid, integrated aspects of a healthy community. For example, the Sadducees' emphasis on prosperity needed to be shaken by active Pharisees, contemplative Essenes and rebel Samaritans who were willing to risk reform. But these four religious types cannot offer their gifts and harmoniously balance each other until the pain of their wounded inner child is healed. Chapters 3 through 6 explore how we can heal childhood patterns of handling shame—patterns that today may make us vulnerable to spiritual abuse and religious addiction. The last chapter in this section, Chapter 7, discusses how these patterns of shame and experiences of abuse may have been handed down to us by many generations of our ancestors.

FAMILY ROLES

	Responsible Child	Rebel	Lost Child	Distractor
Name	Hero	Scapegoat	Loner	Clown/Mascot
Often Born	First	Second	Third	Last
Family Addiction	Defending the Family	Negativity in the Family	Escaping from the Family	Bringing Relief through Humor
Scripture Role	Pharisee	Samaritan	Essene	Sadducee
Hears God Saying	Try harder, I'll love you if . . .	Watch out, you'll be punished.	Be quiet, don't bother me.	All is well, make me happy.
Feeling	Anger Turned Within	Anger Turned Outside	Fears the outer world	Fears the inner world
Looks	Good	Bad	Lonely	Friendly
Seeks	Success	Negative Attention	A Safe Place	Comic Relief
Traps	Workaholism, Legalism, Perfectionism	Substance Addictions, Negativity, Acting Out	Fantasy, Passivity, Food Addiction	Fun, Suicide, Hyperactivity
Gift	Leader (e.g., Peter)	Reformer (e.g., Catherine of Siena)	Creating a Home (e.g., prodigal)	Joy (e.g., St. Francis)
Prayer	Intercession	Confrontation	Contemplation	Praise

3

The Responsible Pharisee

A man in his eighties was once asked the secret of his enormous stamina.

"Well," he answered, "I don't drink. I don't smoke. And I swim a mile a day."

"But I had an uncle who did exactly that, and he died at the age of sixty."

"Ah, the trouble with your uncle was that he didn't do it long enough."[1]

The Responsible Child

The man in his 80's was likely the hero-responsible child who grew up believing that he could do anything if he just tried harder. When the responsible child breaks a cup and feels ashamed, he or she thinks, "I need to try harder and be more careful." These children deal with shame by turning anger inside and striving to be model "good" children. Unlike their rebel siblings, they tend to obey and don't get into trouble. They are addicted to defending the family, and feel compelled to make the family look good. They may become perfectionists, addicted to doing things well, such as getting A's or being a star athlete. If they can shine in some way, they can bury shame and other painful feelings under the accolades and success. The responsible child tends to help, fix things, and do them "because if I don't, no one else will." They are therefore called "the alerts" because they are alert to turn off the lights and to lock the door others forget. More often than not, the oldest child assumes this role because he/she is given more responsibilities than the younger ones. Girls are also socialized into this role as they are taught that women care for others, even at expense to themselves (i.e., girls are taught to be codependent). As adults they tend to enter the helping professions where they can continue to be responsible. One shocking study concluded that 83% of the nurses surveyed were the first-born child of an alcoholic.[2] Grownup responsible children fill our workshops because they are always trying to improve themselves or wanting to learn how to help others.

As with every type, no responsible child exhibits all the above traits. For example, the compulsion to be good may not always extend into being better (outdoing others) or best (perfectionism). For some, the desire to be a good helper may keep them from trying to outdo others. But all responsible children share a basic push to cover shame by being both good and responsible. Their good actions look loving but their swallowed anger (about neglecting their own needs) often wishes others were doing more. As adults their addictive religious pattern tends to be the Pharisee: be good by responsibly keeping the rules, cover shame by more good actions designed to win praise, and earn God's love by striving for perfection. It is easy for me (Matt) to write this because I am the oldest, responsible child. I have almost all the above traits. Even as I type this page, I am aware of how much more there is to say to be complete and how hard it is to say it perfectly. I just threw out twenty pages that didn't measure up!

The Pharisee: The Responsible Child

The Pharisees often seemed to act like myself and other responsible children. The Pharisees began as lay reformers who objected to the priests limiting revelation only to the Pentateuch (the first five books of the Old Testament). They wanted to include all of life, from the severe prophets to the jubilant psalms. Because they wanted to make all of life a worship of God, they stressed keeping all 613 precepts of the law. To be sure they kept all of the law, the Pharisees also tried to keep all the practices of the oral tradition surrounding the law. Thus, what was originally intended as a loving response to God became an unnecessary burden focusing on external ways to be good and earn God's love.

The New Testament has 96 references to Pharisees. Most describe the traits of the responsible child trying to be externally good at the expense of genuine loving. Such Pharisees are addicted to obeying every letter of the extended law perfectly and to looking good to others (Mt 23:5–7). As hypocrites they wash the outside of the cup while leaving the inside dirty. They ostentatiously tithe everything to God but find legalistic ways to avoid giving anything to their poor parents. The Pharisee, addicted to his own righteousness, prays, "O God, I thank you that I am not like the rest of humanity . . ." and names all his good deeds (Lk 18:11). Pharisees spiritually abuse others by imposing, in God's name, burdensome laws regarding everything from handwashing (Lk 11:38) to fasting (Mt 9:14). They behave like their God who scowls and says, "You *should* . . . try harder, be more obedient. . . ." The Pharisee acts out of "I should" (to earn God's love) rather than "I want to" (because God already loves me).[3]

I have much of the Pharisee in me. I surprised no one when as the good, responsible child I became the good, responsible Jesuit priest. I joined the Jesuits because I, like Dennis, thought religious life was the highest calling. The Jesuits also had the best training, and I liked their perfectionistic motto, "*All* for the *greater* glory of God." My formation added to this. Our training emphasized pushing ourselves to be better, even to washing pots as fast as we could. I felt superior because I could give six haircuts in an hour while others lovingly sculpted only one head. One man quit the novitiate after I had scalped him to the bone. He probably had to wear a hat for six months. Even today, I still admire the driven Jesuit who accomplishes great works rather than the peaceful one who does less but with more love. Our founder, St. Ignatius, warned us that "the good (responsible children) are tempted by the good." For example, responsible children are tempted to do more praying, studying, working, and helping the needy (and all of it better than previously) until they collapse. I became addicted to doing every religious action better: prayer, writing religious books (revising my revised versions until the publishing deadline), and improving my retreats on the healing of perfectionism.

Because I addictively used religion to cover shame by looking good, I was vulnerable to anyone who told me a religious way to be better, no matter how spiritually abusive. For example, as Dennis mentioned, in our Jesuit novitiate we were encouraged to whip our bodies. Like my companions, I obeyed because I saw this as another way to be better. It never occurred to me that this was an abusive practice. Many years later, when a friend questioned the healthiness of whipping myself, I instinctively reacted by at first defending those who encouraged the practice. Just as I was addicted to my nuclear family and felt compelled to make it look good, I was also addicted to my church family and felt compelled to defend it.

Because I had the God of the Pharisees, whose love had to be earned, my image of God only reinforced my vulnerability to religious addiction and spiritual abuse. I related to God in the same shame-based way (as a responsible child) that I learned in my family. Each of the four childhood roles can lead to a distorted way of relating to God out of shame. Moreover, our distorted image of God prevents us from receiving the healing love of God that might free us from the cycle of addiction and abuse. As long as I had a God who was asking me to whip myself in order

to be better, I could not find the God who wanted to stroke me
with healing love.

The Gifted Side of the Pharisee

Each of the religious addictive types also has a gifted side, as
does every addiction. Writing to Bill W., the founder of A.A., Dr.
Carl Jung said that the more he listened to the stories of alcoholics, the more he understood that alcoholism was a longing for
spiritus or Spirit: "Alcohol in Latin is *spiritus* and you use the
same word for the highest religious experience as well as for the
most depraving poison."[4] The alcoholic has a gift for religious
experience.

What then is the gift under the Pharisee's drive for perfection?
The Pharisees of Jesus' time are not spoken of very positively in the
scriptures, because of the later persecution of Christians by the
Pharisees' successors. Yet Paul is proud to call himself a Pharisee
(Phil 3:5–6), because the Pharisee has a hunger for holiness, a
longing to be closer to God in every action. This positive side leads
Nicodemus (a Pharisee) to use his gifts as an obedient, responsible
child to defend Jesus before the council, observing that the law
demanded that the accused have a hearing (Jn 7:50). Peter, too, is a
responsible child. He wants to be the first to walk on water, the first
to claim that he would follow Jesus to his death, and the first to
defend Jesus by cutting off a soldier's ear.

Jesus sees the gifts of caring and leadership under Peter's
drive to always take responsibility. Contrary to his desire to be first
in following Jesus, Peter denies him three times. Then when
Jesus on the lakeshore asks Peter three times "Do you love me?"
Peter's triple denial is healed and he can finally be loved at his
worst (Jn 21:1–23). Once Peter can be loved at his worst, Jesus
can give him the leadership responsibility of "Feed my lambs,
feed my sheep." To the degree a responsible child can receive love

instead of compulsively trying to earn love, that person can give love by caring for others.[5]

Discovering the Root Negative Memories

The responsible child/Pharisee role comes from choices we made in the midst of hurts that filled us with shame. When during an early hurt did we say to ourselves, "I will try harder and be more responsible"? On the other hand, we may have been hurt and said, "I will not be responsible again," and now have difficulty taking responsibility. Earlier memories often have more impact, but any memory in which we still feel pain and shame is affecting us. The developmental psychologist Erik Erikson stresses the grade school years as the key time we form the responsible child who wants to do things well.

My earliest memory of a hurt in which I chose to be the responsible child is when I was about two years old. Newborn Dennis was getting all the attention. My way to get attention was to find a pillow for my dad's noon nap on the davenport when he came home from work. The pillow was bigger than I was, but I can still feel my pride in being a responsible helper. Every visitor came to hug Dennis first and me last. By getting my dad's pillow as soon as he came in the door, I got his first hug. As he took the pillow, he also praised me for being so thoughtful.

My most painful memory of choosing to be a responsible child happened when I was seven and my brother John was two. One day John began breathing with a wheezing sound and we thought he had a bad cold. We were afraid to take John to the doctor in the cold weather. I kept telling my worried mother that John would be o.k. Finally, the neighboring nurse came and told my mother to call an ambulance. John died of a collapsed windpipe five minutes from the hospital. I loved John, and in my role of older brother I felt responsible for his death. I was sure my mother would have called the nurse five minutes earlier if I hadn't told her not to worry. Maybe all the times I wrestled John with headlocks had weakened his windpipe. When my parents told me that God took John to heaven so he could be happier, I remembered all those fights. I thought, "If I had made John happier here, God would not have had to take him away." I made the Pharisee's inner vow, "I will try harder so nothing bad happens again. If only I had been more responsible, John would be alive."

I also learned how to be a responsible Pharisee from our Irish pastor, Fr. Daly. As an altar boy, I dreaded serving Mass because he always had a stern, correcting word. If we went out walking too fast or too slow, with our hands folded too much up or down, or looking at anyone, we would get a lecture after Mass on being more reverent. If we prayed too fast, especially the Pater Noster (Our Father), he would slow us all down. If I twisted my tongue over, "ad Deum qui laetificat juventutem meum," he would publicly repeat the right response while those in the congregation watched my red face and got ready for my next mistake. He also expected perfection of himself. He would start over (his record was five times) if he didn't pronounce perfectly every syllable of the consecration. If we didn't put the missal at the precise angle for the gospel, he would correct it. If anyone tried to sneak out before he left the altar, he would turn around and command them to return to their pew. I envisioned God with the stern face and gray hair of Fr. Daly. In imposing upon me his own harsh and demanding image of God, Fr. Daly was spiritually abusing me.

My other memory of trying harder as the result of a hurt with a religious figure occurred in seventh grade. I was chosen to represent my school on Fr. Gales' television program. The honor of the school rode on me, so my teacher released me from a week's afternoon classes to study Fr. Gales' topic, the Immaculate Conception. But on live television my thoughts got all scrambled and I mistakenly said that the Immaculate Conception freed Jesus (it was Mary) from sin. After I explained this mystery for three minutes, Fr. Gales interrupted and straightened it all out. Trying to save face, I said, "That's what I meant to say." I had disgraced myself and my school in front of everyone on TV. The next day the nun who was my teacher glared at me and said in front of all my classmates, "Any fool can say 'That's what I meant to say.' " I can still see her steely gray eyes glaring behind wire-rimmed glasses and shooting bullets that could have stopped a hurricane. I made forty inner vows never to be unprepared again. For years afterward, I had difficulty looking people in the eye when they wore wire-rimmed glasses.

Discovering Our Positive Healing Memories

Such negative memories can be healed by taking in love from positive memories. Recovering alcoholics continue to tell their recovery stories at A.A. meetings so the memories that helped them recover become alive and empowering once again. A.A. members carry an anniversary "chip" (medallion) in their pockets, so if they get tempted to drink, they can touch it and remember their years of sobriety.

Since my responsible child tries to earn love by more perfection rather than by first receiving love that empowers a loving response, I need to soak in memories of unconditional love. My two-year-old child carrying the pillow still longs for my dad's hug. I simply go back to receiving a hug in that memory or recall another memory where I got a hug for who I was rather than for what I did. I remember when I dented our car and my dad simply hugged me and said, "I am glad that you didn't get hurt. We can always repair the car." I also remember when he drove me to enter the novitiate and said goodbye. With tears in his eyes, he gave me a final hug and said, "Remember the house key is hanging in the garage. You are always welcome back no matter what you do."

My inner child who was once a controlled altar boy wants to be spontaneously himself with God. I go back to memories such as dancing during a Mass held in the garbage dump of Juarez. The garbage dump was the opposite of Fr. Daly's spotless church with the missal at its precise, correct angle. I also get healed each time I sing songs of praise and move with my whole body in free gestures.

As for my seventh grade TV fiasco, years later in my imagination I simply put Jesus in the classroom, felt my shame and looked into his loving eyes. He said that he was proud of me to risk going on TV when I was only twelve. He told my teacher and classmates to cast their stones only if they were without fault. He then told my teacher that the real problem was not that her pupil made a mistake, since students must risk errors in order to learn. Her real problem was that her reputation was at stake as my teacher who didn't teach me well enough about the Immaculate Conception. Finally Jesus told me what I had forgotten: she was upset because her name was Sr. Mary Immaculata! Then she turned red. After that, I could look people in the eye who wore wire-rimmed glasses. I also could appear on TV without the fear that I would have nothing to say or make a big blunder.

The Responsible Child Can Be Healed

I know that the responsible child can be healed because mine continues to heal year by year. Perhaps the greatest healing came when I finally dealt with the hurt of John's death. At age eighteen I began my Jesuit life with a thirty day retreat and a general confession. I found myself mentioning three areas of sin and then something I had not even written: "I also blame myself for my brother John's death." Rivers of healing tears choked off more words. Finally I had surfaced my most shameful secret that I had kept even from myself. Joe, the novice master, threw his arms around me and said, "God loves you more than ever and I do too." I knew for the first time that I was loved at my worst. With that love I forgave myself. I wrote in my diary, "I feel like a cement tomb has cracked open and I am finally free." My responsible Pharisee was no longer saying, "I will try harder so nothing like this happens again." My responsible child was no longer responsible for anything but receiving God's love.

HEALING PROCESS

Perhaps you also might want to invite Jesus or your higher power into a painful memory, as Matt did with Sr. Mary Immaculata. Psychologists tell us that whatever we imagine deeply enough to be felt affects us as much as if we really experienced it. You have probably already used your imagination in this way if, for example, you have ever day-dreamed about a vacation you wanted to take and savored it in your imagination before you even left home.

---

1. Let yourself be flooded by memories of those who hugged you in a way that felt good (grandparents, friends, a special teacher, etc.).

2. Get in touch with a painful memory. Experience the feelings and share them with Jesus or your higher power.

3. Let the loving, caring presence you felt in those hugs fill whatever memory of hurt has surfaced. Let yourself feel the pain and how you are loved in it without having to change it.

4. You may wish to ask others to give you what you need. I still collect hugs from my dad and other healthy father figures.

4

The Rebel Samaritan

During World War II, when the Nazis invaded Denmark, they ordered all the Jews to wear yellow stars on their sleeves. The next morning the ruler of Denmark, King Christian, rode out on his horse. He had put a yellow star on his sleeve. The Danish people followed his example, and they too put on yellow stars. Thus they rebelled against the Nazis and protected the Jews.

The Rebel Child

King Christian and his people were healthy rebels. The wounded rebel deals with shame by expressing anger directly as the "difficult child." His or her anger can also be indirect, through passive-aggressive behavior such as not listening, not following directions, teasing others, being late, or taking unhealthy risks. Often the rebel is the second child who chooses the role of being bad because she or he can't compete with the first child who is being good. When the cup breaks, the rebel might say, "Who cares? They are always picking on me." That strong willed attitude in turn provokes caretakers to further try to control the rebel. This further reinforces the rebel's belief that adults are police saying, "Don't. . . ." The rebel serves the dysfunctional family by being the "problem child" or "scapegoat." This child, who expresses the conflict no one else wants to face, is addicted to the negativity in the family. Unfortunately, families often try to change the child rather than the root family problem (e.g., alcoholism, poor communication, etc.) that is abusing the child and fueling his or her way of handling shame. If this abuse is unhealed, then the child may find a way of abusing others in turn, and may even have brushes with the law.[1] If healed, this child can stand up to anything and becomes the creative nonconformist marching to an inner drumbeat. Such rebels lead revolutions. MIT science historian Frank Sulloway found that twenty-three out of the twenty-eight major scientific revolutions were led by later-born children. On the other hand those with the least rebel in them, namely the first-born, responsible children, have almost no scientific revolutions to their credit.[2]

The Samaritan Rebel

The Samaritans were originally Jews who intermarried with Gentiles and remained faithful to Yahweh. But most other Jews considered the Samaritans heretical schismatics. For one thing, not all the Samaritans were exiled (720 BC) and so were not "tried and true" Jews. They also refused to rigidly obey Jewish laws. For instance, they intermarried with "pagans." Because the Samaritans were faithful to Yahweh, when the Jerusalem Jews returned from exile (537 BC), the Samaritans volunteered to help rebuild the Jerusalem temple. But Nehemiah and the Jerusalem Jews responsible for rebuilding the temple turned down the Samaritans' offer. The message was clear, "Because you Samaritans haven't lived the Jerusalem way, you are not really Jews." Nehemiah forbade intermarriage between Jews and Samaritans, and he broke up existing mixed marriages. The Samaritans rebelled. They temporarily blocked the temple construction. Then they attempted to assassinate

Nehemiah. Finally they built their own temple to Yahweh in Samaria at Mt. Gerizim. The gift of the Samaritan and the rebel child is that they fight so that neither religion nor anyone else can take away from them their ability to feel what they feel, think what they think, and trust what they trust. But they also have a dark side. The Samaritan and the rebel child often appear bad because they may respond to pain by hurting others in the same way that they were hurt. In Jesus' time, the Samaritans spiritually abused others by profaning the Jerusalem temple with dead bones and regularly attacking pilgrims. Jesus experienced their hostility when journeying to Jerusalem (Lk 9:52). The rebel tends toward an attack stance of being "against." This may range from the Samaritan's active hostility that fights against religion, to an aversion addiction that compulsively avoids religious practices.[3] Often this happens because the re-

bel identifies God and religious authorities with parents who were seen as over-controlling.

The Gift Side of the Samaritan

On the other hand, Jesus commended the Good Samaritan for violating the religious prohibitions against touching anyone who might be dead (Lk 10:25, Num 19:11). Perhaps the Good Samaritan violated those prohibitions because as a rebel receiving abuse, he had compassion for the man abused and lying on the road. Or perhaps the Good Samaritan stopped because a rebel is a nonconformist who takes risks to change what needs to be changed. The Samaritan woman (Jn 4) is another rebel at home with violating religious customs. She has been married five times, talks alone to a Jewish man, and even chooses to believe in him as the Messiah. Like the Good Samaritan, the Samaritan woman is a conscientious objector who places the higher law of love above obedience to religious authority. In sending her to preach to others, Jesus chooses this conscientious objector to be his witness, in a culture that forbade women to be legal witnesses.

In speaking with the Samaritan woman and asking for a drink, Jesus too is a conscientious objector. As the scripture scholar Joachim Jeremias points out, Samaritan women were considered "as menstruants from the cradle," and therefore always religiously unclean.[4] Because of this, any place that a Samaritan woman touched was unclean, as was food or drink that had accidentally touched that place for even a second. Rabbi Eliezer said, "He who eats the bread of a Samaritan is like one who eats the flesh of swine." Thus Jesus is not only going against the customs of his culture by talking with a strange woman (especially a Samaritan), but he is also breaking religious laws by asking her for a drink.

We normally think of conscientious objection as disobedience to a literal law, for the sake of obeying our conscience. However, it seems to us that the term "conscientious objection" can also be used in a metaphorical sense, to describe any situation in which we resist institutional pressure for the sake of obeying our conscience. The courage to resist in this way is the gift side of the rebel and of the Samaritan. It's a gift that we need today.

We recently heard a story of a parish in New England that used this gift and participated in an act of conscientious objection similar to that for which Jesus commended the Samaritans. This parish had a very progressive pastor who worked cooperatively with the parishioners. The parish community was so healthy and vital that people came from long distances to participate in it. Without consulting the community, the local chancery transferred the pastor and assigned another to take his place. The new pastor's style was highly authoritarian. For example, on Sunday mornings before Mass he stood at the front door of the church and asked worshippers where they lived. When he discovered people who came from other parishes, he told them to go home. The community decided they could not work well with the new pastor, and feared that all the good they had accomplished with his predecessor would be destroyed. They gathered together and decided to withhold their donations to the parish. The chancery got the message and replaced the new pastor with someone more acceptable to the parishioners. The chancery also modified its policy of transferring pastors, to include more consultation with local communities.

The rebel's gift of conscientious objection that the New England parishioners practiced has a long history. Early Christians practiced conscientious objection against the state by refusing military service. In our time, Dorothy Day's paper, *The Catholic Worker*, spearheaded a peace movement responsible for legalizing conscientious objection during the Vietnam War. For centuries, from the early Christians to Dorothy Day, the Church has tried to provide a safe environment for the rebel conscientious objector protesting against unjust *civil* laws and authorities. The chancery in New England gives us hope that the Church can provide that same safe environment for conscientious objectors protesting against unjust *religious* authority.[5]

When there is no safe environment for healthy conscientious objection, rebellion may be expressed through passive aggressive behavior, i.e., covertly rather than straightforwardly. Examples might be dropping out of a Christian community without ever explaining why, reporting someone to a bishop or other authority without first confronting that person directly, or Catholic priests secretly acting out sexually rather than openly confronting the rule of mandatory celibacy.

The Samaritan woman in John 4 is a model of how Jesus provides a safe environment in which the rebel's gifts can be discovered. Jesus begins the conversation by respecting the woman as a person who has something to give him. He says to her, "Give me a drink." He then turns her argument on where to worship into a dialogue and speaks to her thirst for more life. Perhaps Jesus appreciated rebels because he was so much of one himself. He placed love over law to heal on the sabbath, touch unclean lepers and stop the legal stoning of an adulterous woman.

I (Matt) have too little of the rebel child and Samaritan in me. My responsible child learned well to stamp out any rebellious stirrings within me. I am uncomfortable with the angry, rebel Jesus cleansing the temple or confronting church authorities as "whited sepulchers" because of their addiction to unjust church law (Mt 23:13–39). William Sloane Coffin, Jr. writes,

> Jesus was angry over 50% of the time, and it's very dangerous theology to try to improve on Jesus. The anger needs to be focused, but anger is what maintains your sanity. Anger keeps you from tolerating the intolerable.[6]

Unlike myself, church reformers like St. Catherine of Siena seemed comfortable expressing Jesus' rebellious anger. In speaking to a group of erring cardinals about their unjust laws, she called them "not sweet-smelling flowers, but corruptions which cause the whole world to stink." In 1376, Catherine even confronted Pope Gregory XI and persuaded him to leave Avignon and return to Rome to begin reform.[7]

As the shortest kid, if I had expressed my anger as Catherine did, I would have come out on the short end of any fight. In my family I never learned how to be angry, let alone with God or the Church. I wanted to look good even in situations where rules should be broken. Before signing petitions confronting abuse in the Church and requesting reform, I still raise the question "Is it safe?" before "Is it the right thing to do?" Even as we write this book, I feel frightened to say anything that might upset someone, no matter how true.

At retreats I feel frightened to do anything that might upset someone, no matter how right. For example, for years I strictly followed the letter of the law and permitted only those who recognized the Pope, weren't divorced, or had no serious sin to receive communion. I was denying communion to a part of Christ's mystical body yet claiming in communion that I was becoming one with the whole Christ. I ignored that Jesus gave communion to Judas and that we come as wounded people praying, "Only say the word and I shall be healed."

Today I believe that Eucharist is a healing sacrament to be received as a response to God's love, not a merit badge of God's love earned by enough good actions. The rebel in me wants to set aside the literal law and act upon a higher law of love (Mt 22:34–40). Yet the obedient responsible child in me is afraid to set aside the law. I am tempted to obey out of fear and I find it hard to set aside the law and lovingly invite everyone to communion. I obey out of fear because I do not want to risk the disapproval of bishops and other church authorities. So how do I love with my rebel energy and yet keep my obedient responsible child satisfied? At our retreats when I am asked about communion, I give two rules.

I say, "We have a rule that I cannot publicly invite everyone to receive. Secondly, we have another rule (I smile) that I am not to refuse communion to anyone who comes forward. Do what you believe Jesus wants you to do." I'll bet you can guess what happens. I pray for the day when these pharisaical rules can be set aside. Until then, this is the best I can do because I am still a responsible child in process of getting healed, as is the rest of the Church.

Discovering Our Root Negative Memories

According to Erik Erikson, the developmental stage from age one and a half to three years is the critical time for developing autonomy, the capacity to say "Yes" and "No." If caregivers do not encourage the child to make choices, the child will have either too much or too little of the rebel's capacity to say "No."

I had too little. My earliest memory of this is being spanked at age four for running around the neighborhood with my friend, Lance, who was wearing his mother's huge, pink bloomers. Lance was the neighborhood rebel and any of his rebel influence got spanked out of me. Later Dennis and I did rebel enough to hide the stick Mom used for spankings. We put it in John's old baby carriage. We knew that in her grief over John's death, Mom would never look there.

When I imagine my rebel child saying "No," I recall a memory of how my rebel was put down. I discovered it because I was wondering why I didn't like to shake hands when introduced to others. It wasn't a fear of intimacy, because I was open to giving a hug. Only a handshake felt insincere. As I sat with this feeling, a memory came that fit. I was four years old and two-year-old Dennis had just scribbled up our coloring book. So I hit him and he hit me. My mother was tired of endlessly sorting out who started it. She ordered us to stop fighting and made us tell each other that we were sorry. Then we had to shake hands. I remember squeezing Dennis' hand as hard as I could because I was still angry that he didn't get punished and that my righteousness wasn't vindicated. I had to swallow my angry words, "It's not fair! He started it!" To get even, I robbed Dennis' bank. As I share extensively in *Belonging,* what helped me with this hurt was a written dialogue where Jesus surprised me by supporting both our rebel kids and saying:

> As a two-year-old, Dennis is always looking for another way to assert himself. He doesn't listen when you tell him he can't color it. That just makes him want to do it. You should be angry. You have a right to try solving things your way and see if it works rather than always be forced to shake hands.

To have power, memories do not have to be early family memories. I still think twice about confronting Church authorities because of a confrontation with my Jesuit provincial back in 1966. I have had excellent provincials and superiors except for this one. He was finally removed because he was mentally ill. By that time he had thrown many of my classmates out of the Jesuits. He tried to do the same with me. I had just sent Dennis some pamphlets on scripture, since he was teaching catechism. I didn't realize they were written by Protestants, whose writing would be accepted only after Vatican II. My provincial came across these pamphlets and told me that I obviously was more serious about being a Protestant than a Jesuit. I was therefore out of the Jesuits. In shock I told him that I had no idea the pamphlets were forbidden and wanted another chance. So he put me on probation. I could be a Jesuit if I behaved. That reinforced my good responsible child, undermined any rebel in me and left me fearing even healthy authorities. Fortunately, he is gone and I am still around as a Jesuit!

Rediscovering Our Positive Memories

Perhaps my reluctant rebel has been healed most by rubbing shoulders with healthy rebels and catching their gift. For example, Dennis, Sheila and I spent three weeks living in Nicaragua with Steve, a Jesuit classmate. This was when our C.I.A. was supporting the Contras and Archbishop Obando y Bravo and his wealthy supporters against the Sandinistas. As an economist, Steve had uncovered U.S. involvement in Church corruption. He sided with the poor. Because of this he was on death lists and had to travel under assumed names. Yet he fearlessly spoke the truth. We caught his prophetic zeal and in 1988 we gave retreats to both sides in Nicaragua's war zone, while shots lit up the sky every night.

Positive memories of those who have stood up for me also restore my rebel. In 1974 some leaders of the Catholic Charismatic Renewal refused to sell our book *Healing of Memories* because they thought recalling painful memories was dangerous. Francis MacNutt, however, stood up for us. He spoke to these charismatic leaders on our behalf and asked us not to take their reaction as a reason to stop. He told us our book was good, and encouraged us to keep writing for those who were open to the integration of spirituality and psychology. Next to 6'4" Francis, who was the expert on healing, Dennis and I felt ourselves growing taller. Because Francis stood up for us, we in turn grew a little more rebel backbone to defend ourselves or another. When we get shaky, we return to memories like these to get strength.

The Rebel Child Can Be Healed

A major step in healing all three of our reluctant rebel children occurred when Linda came to us for prayer for healing of childhood sexual abuse. We thought Jesus' priority would be to help Linda forgive the men who abused her. As Linda recalled the scene of her abuse, she could see Jesus with her there. However, she remained unable to forgive. Linda had enough healthy rebel that she was unwilling to pretend forgiveness in order to please us or God.

We (Sheila & Dennis) then sensed that Jesus was not first of all asking Linda to forgive. Instead Jesus shared Linda's anger. He was outraged over the desecration of her body, just as he was outraged over the desecration of God's temple (Jn 2:13–17). As we shared this with Linda, Linda saw Jesus driving out the people who abused her, just as he drove out the money changers who desecrated the temple. Linda then began to cry for the first time in fourteen years. She told us the reason she was crying:

> That Jesus would get so angry for me . . . that he would love
> me so much. He just wants to share all of me. If I am crying,
> he will cry. If I am happy, he will be happy.

In this prayer, Jesus gave Linda what she needed most: to know how much he loved her in the midst of her hurt and anger, and even to know that her anger was Jesus' anger. For the next few weeks Linda didn't even try to forgive. Instead she continued to feel her anger and allow Jesus to be angry on her behalf. Eventually as Linda began to trust that she was loved in her hurt and anger, she began to forgive her relatives and herself. Today she works as a therapist with families who suffer from sexual abuse. [8]

Linda changed our image of God. Rebellious anger is for us no longer something to be rid of but a way of meeting God. Jesus rebelling in the temple and being loved by God in that rebellion is now a key image we use when praying with people who flee their own anger. Such people can be with their own anger when they see how Jesus is with them in it. In this way, their anger naturally resolves itself and eventually they move to forgiveness.

Several years ago Linda led us to address the healing of sexual abuse. Now, in this book, we are addressing the healing of spiritual abuse. This has been difficult for the responsible Pharisee in all three of us, who wants to look good even to those who abuse us. As we struggle to develop some healthy rebel within ourselves, we understand the fear that often tempts Church authorities to crush rebels. We want to be approved of by others rather than be rebels pointing out their abusive patterns. Thanks to Linda, we are now writing this wih her conviction that Jesus can heal whatever abuse is discovered.

HEALING PROCESS

1. See yourself as a child, at a time when you were hurt and angry. Perhaps you were blamed for something you didn't do, such as starting a fight. Where are you? What are you wearing? Doing? Saying? How do you feel? (Hurt, misunderstood, ashamed, guilty, fearful, etc.?)

2. In writing, share what is in your heart with God as you understand God. Write as if you were writing a love letter to your best friend, sharing what you feel most deeply. Don't worry about having the "right" words, but only try to share your heart. If drawing is more helpful for you than writing, draw a picture or symbol to express what you feel.

3. Now get in touch with God's response to you, as he/she is already speaking to you within. You might do this by asking what are the most loving words that you could possibly hear, or by imagining that what you have just shared is a note or drawing for you from the person you love most and you want to respond to that person in the most loving possible way.

4. Write (or draw) God's response. Perhaps it will be just one word or one sentence. You can be sure that anything you write (or draw) which helps you to know that you are loved is really from God.

5

The Lost Essene

When I was little I was sick once, and I wanted something, only I didn't know what it was. My father sat by my bed and talked to me.

"I want," I said.

"I know, Twink."

"What do I want?"

"Everything, Twink."

"Can I have it?"

"Yes."

"When?"

"Just as soon as you're better."

"Right now?"

"In a little while."

"Tomorrow?"

"Tomorrow for sure."

"What will everything be?"

"You, Twink. You'll get yourself back the minute you're better. You'll forget you ever lost yourself. And that'll be everything."

"Is that all? Just me?"

"Yes, Twink. That's all there is."

"But I've always got me, Papa."

"Except now, because you're sick. Because when anybody's sick, he loses himself—but just for a little while. That's what sickness is. All of a sudden you're not

*there anymore, so of course you want—you want all
kinds of things—everything—but what you really want
is always yourself, because if you've got love, that's all
there is—yourself and love, and I love you, Twink."*[1]

The Lost Child

The lost child often feels the neediness and loss of self that
Twink felt when sick. Such a child feels alone even when in a
crowd. When breaking a cup, this child wants to run away from
the shame-filled scene. Her parents typically say, "Mary isn't a
problem (unlike the rebel). You would hardly know that Mary is
around." Mary is often a middle child who is overlooked as
attention focuses on the responsible child who excels, the naugh-
ty child who rebels or the cute, youngest child. She has fewer
photos in the family album, fewer friends, and doesn't like to
stand out in school. The name "lost child" is fitting, because this
child often has an aura of loss and grief. Perhaps because she is so
sensitive to loss, Mary's world is full of fear and she becomes
adroit at adjusting and avoiding conflict. She finds it difficult to
ask for what she needs.

The lost child is addicted to escaping from the family. Thus,
she withdraws into her own fantasy world and can spend endless
hours playing alone with her dolls, watching television, quietly
reading books, or wandering in nature. If this pattern continues,
the lost child becomes the shy introvert who quietly lives unnoti-
ced. As an adult Mary doesn't like loud parties and feels more comfortable talking to one person rather than mixing with everyone.

The Essene: Fearful Withdrawal from the Evil World

The lost child may become the Essene who fearfully withdraws from the shaming, evil world into a desert utopia.[2] The

Essenes lived out the lost child's ideal of avoiding conflict and being as ordinary as possible, in a protective community that discouraged individuality. They lived frugally, sharing a common treasury, table, and uniform clothing so no one would stand out. They worked in lonely fields and silently copied or studied the manuscripts later found in the Qumran library. As the mystical "children of light," they withdrew from the outside world of the "children of darkness." Their leaders, claiming special knowledge of God's will, predicted a coming apocalyptic battle which the community would survive by obeying the leaders. These leaders, who governed by divine authority, were placed on a pedestal in a privileged caste and had to undergo cleansing if touched by a follower. Thus community members were isolated even from their leaders.

The Essenes were fearful of mixing with others in the Jerusalem temple. Thus they substituted their own rites for temple sacrifice. The Essenes declined in numbers until their end in 66–70 AD, when Rome stamped out all Jewish sects. Why the decline? Some blame their rule of celibacy that left no heirs. But other religious communities thrive for centuries with celibacy. A more likely explanation is that what started as a rich experience of community religious life degenerated into a rigidity that demanded blind obedience to practices that stamped out individual initiative and gifts. Essenes who disobeyed were expelled or punished by having food withheld until they were forced to live on grass. There are stories of how Essenes became so dependent on the community that ejected members starved because they had taken an oath not to eat common food.[3] We know little more about them, because they took a cult-like oath not to reveal their secrets, even under torture.

In such an addictive cult structure that stamps out individual personality, members feel lost and passively dependent. Cults don't usually attract healthy new members, and eventually can lead to destruction as quickly as Jonestown disappeared when hundreds dependently followed their leader, James Jones, in drinking poison. Groups such as Jonestown or the Branch Davidians in Waco, Texas can create followers who act as lost children rather than as active, contributing adults.

The Essenes illustrate how the lost child is susceptible to religious addiction and spiritual abuse. Their susceptibity to such addiction and abuse is caused especially by their fears of conflict and of involvement in the outer world. For example, lost children may become addicted to the mystical dimension of religion. Healthy prayer connects us to the outer world. Wounded lost children may use prayer addictively, to explore the mystery under the mystery of every mystery, i.e., to escape from the outer world.

Lost children can also become addicted to religious authority, passively cooperating in order to avoid conflict. Thus, they are vulnerable to spiritually abusive religious authorities, as I

(Sheila) was to the leaders of the San Francisco community, especially those who encourage martyrdom and long-suffering obedience. Lost children tend to listen to authorities and take them seriously, without expecting authorities to listen to them and take them seriously. Their God is no help, because he/she may resemble their distant parents. Thus, they may not expect God to listen to them or take them seriously either. By cooperating with abusive authority rather than confronting it, lost children may contribute to abusive structures. In order to avoid conflict, they can become spiritual abusers themselves, as they say "Yes" to abusive leaders instead of outspokenly standing in solidarity with victims.

The Gift Side of the Essene

What are the gifts of the Essene? The healthy Essene is a contemplative who can listen in solitude. As a natural introvert, the Essene can access and discern interior movements more readily than the busy extrovert. The historian Arnold Toynbee pointed out what was common to all the great world leaders in the civilizations he studied. They had the habit of withdrawing to where they could listen deeply, discern wisely, and dream of new possibilities. The Essene is a natural day dreamer who, with the creative gifts of the intuitive, apprehends what eludes others.

The Essene's withdrawal balances the active stance of the responsible Pharisee. I (Matt) need to be open to the gifts of the lost child that my responsible child pushes aside. If it were up to my unhealed responsible child, I would reverse how Jesus decided to live a hidden (Essene) life for thirty years and to work for only three. My growing edge is the lost child's side of contemplatively BEING and receiving rather than my responsible child's side of actively DOING and giving. The ideal is the lost prodigal son, who in his aloneness and grief discovers that his deepest desire is to go home to where he can receive greater life.

Discovering the Root Negative Memories

Experiences of isolation that were painful and shaming stifled my lost child. For example, as the shortest kid, I was the last one chosen for games, the first one caught in tag, and the most defenseless one in any fight. The game I dreaded most was "keep away." The person in the middle has the choice to either catch a ball that two persons throw back and forth over him or her, or to tag one of those persons before the ball is thrown again. Being short, I couldn't run fast enough to tag the person or leap high enough to catch the ball. Thus I was forever in the middle. I was stuck in isolation and mocked for it.

Erik Erikson stresses the first two years as the key time we form the capacity to trust the world. Otherwise, we may fearfully distrust and withdraw. For example, I recall when I was about that age, my mother had just baked my favorite cookie, chocolate chip. She let me pick out the two biggest cookies and told me, "Now that's all. I don't want you spoiling your dinner." Then she went to answer the phone. The newly baked cookies tasted twice as good as old ones. They were also ten times better than dinner, so I took another cookie while she wasn't looking. The phone call was a wrong number and my mother returned quickly. She caught me with a half-eaten third cookie. She scolded me for disobeying and told me to stay in my room until dinner. A similar scenario happened often, and I began to connect being ashamed with going off to be alone in my room. Since isolation was my mother's way of punishment, even as an adult I often didn't like staying in my room. I became conscious of this years later, when I asked myself why I never liked to pray in my room. I was always going outside or to a different room. In my room I felt more distant from God, who seemed like my disciplining mother. Now that I've uncovered and worked through memories of being punished through isolation in my room, I can pray, study or be in my room alone without feeling uncomfortable.

Discovering Our Positive Healing Memories

The Vatican I Church of my childhood taught me to rely on religious authorities and not on my inner experience. This changed when I learned to trust my quiet, inner, alone self with the help of my novice master, Joe Sheehan. I would ask him to solve problems for me. But Joe never told me the answer. Instead he always asked me, "What do you think?" I found myself expressing new thoughts and coming up with solutions. Then Joe would chime in, "That's better than what I could have told you. Trust yourself." He taught me the Ignatian way of trusting my deepest self and what it knows and desires as the way to God.

Who was comfortable with being the lost child and could make me feel at home with mine? My cousin, Sister Mary Jane Linn, comes to mind. She had an active career directing St. Catherine's College nursing program. Then she retired and worked full time interceding for our ministry. When she was quietly praying for us at healing retreats, people experienced much healing. When we were snarled in obstacles, we would check later and find it was the time when she had stopped praying to take a break. The time she returned from her break turned out to be the same time the healing process had resumed again. She not only gave me confidence in the power of being alone with God in prayer, but I absorbed her capacity for solitude just by being with her. She had a peaceful, quiet stillness that crept into me as we took walks and she said almost nothing. When I was with her, the gifts of the Essene grew in me. I could peacefully BE rather than frantically DO. Later her ministry shifted to helping her elderly sisters die peacefully, probably because they, like myself, caught her inner stillness. She shared her positive memories of this Essene-like ministry in *Healing the Dying*.[4]

The Lost Child Can Be Healed

My lost child is my feminine side. That's why I need women like Mary Jane teaching me how to BE quietly receptive, rather than charging ahead with my masculine energy to DO everything better regardless of obstacles and limits. Until recently, when I turned to God, it was to the masculine Jesus, Father, or Spirit. At forty-eight, I didn't think I needed to be mothered by God or anyone else.

I learned I did when my eighty-year-old mother began suffering stomach pains. She was also losing her memory. I feared she might have stomach cancer or Alzheimer's disease. We convinced her to see a doctor. In his office she couldn't remember the name of the current President. It would be a week before we would get test results.

I spent that week grieving and preparing for the worst. I was hoping that if my mother had Alzheimer's, she would also have stomach cancer. That way she would die quickly before losing her mind and turning into a demented vegetable. I realized how much I would miss my mother as a friend if she lost her mind and couldn't really be present. I would miss her weekly letters that always end with how much she loves me and how lucky she was to marry my father. I would miss her especially on St. Patrick's Day, when we celebrate the Irish faith and "it could be worse" side she gave me. She lived for her children and with my dad would travel hundreds of miles to type one of our manuscripts or to Argentina just to visit us. My parents and I often go out to celebrate with a meal together, and it would be a lonely meal if she were gone. She doesn't say or do much, but loves a lot whether shortening my pants cuffs or making my favorite bacon, lettuce and tomato sandwich. I took a few minutes to breathe in her warm, nurturing love.

As these memories flooded me, I knew I could continue to take in her love as I just had, even when she was present only in memory. I knew this was true because the Irish faith she gave me trusts that in God, love continues forever. At Mass one day I realized that each time I would receive Eucharist, I would be receiving her love in the heart of Jesus. How different it would be to receive Jesus and be loved by my mother. Then it dawned on me that I don't have to wait until my mother dies to receive a mother's love from God. God doesn't become more once my mother dies, but even now has as much love for me as my mother. So I stopped and breathed in as before my mother's love, but this time from God's heart.

It was a whole new experience of God, who never before had been an Irish Mother! I could feel God loving me with my mother's maternal love. My eyes filled with tears at missing her, yet still being loved maternally. I soaked myself in that maternal love that gave birth and life to me. Then I thought, "Stop this, my mother is still alive." But then I heard another inner voice saying, "True, but God is just as much Imma (mother) as Abba (father), so keep soaking up Imma." I did. Before this, I always soaked up a mother's love from Mary. But just as no one can ever take the place of my mother, even though I have many mother figures who love me, so too Mary can never take the place of God's deeper maternal love which created me.

As it turned out, Imma gave me back my mother with a doctor's report of no cancer, no Alzheimer's, and a prescription for B-12 to correct a simple vitamin deficiency. I learned from this experience that for forty-eight years I had lost the feminine side of God. I had also lost much of the feminine side of myself, the gifted side of the lost child who could quietly and receptively BE. (For others the feminine side might be extroverted and talkative.) As Dennis mentioned, we become like the God we adore. As long as I knew only a male God, I overdeveloped the masculine side of myself. And as long as I overdeveloped the masculine side of myself, I perceived God as only male. The more I get to know Imma, the more I recover my feminine lost child.

For example, I just returned from an eight-day retreat where retreatants and staff could sign up for a massage. The massage was provided to help us center interiorly and let go in order to become more receptive. It was far more than that for me. As the sixty-eight-year-old nun massaged me, I felt God's hands massaging life into me. (I had no idea that the same happened to Dennis in his dream described in Chapter 2.) I had felt God's hands massaging life into me previously, but this time they were Imma's feminine hands—delicate, caring, and inviting me to just be a sponge absorbing life. For an hour I soaked up in every muscle Imma's loving caress. I let myself sink into a feminine mode of being and receiving. The next day my six retreatants all had breakthroughs during our conferences. I think it was because after Imma's massage I became twice as receptive to God and to them. Now Imma is not just an Irish Mother but also my Masseuse!

HEALING PROCESS

Are you too much or too little the lost child-Essene? (Do you withdraw to be alone too much or too little?) You might wish to try the following prayer:

1. See Jesus or your higher power standing before you or seated in a rocking chair. See him or her with arms opened to you. Let yourself be welcomed into those arms, letting him or her hold you and perhaps rock you in the chair. Feel those arms around you and let yourself be loved as if you were a small child in its mother's or father's arms.

2. In the safety of those arms, recall one or two negative memories of being hurt and withdrawing in fear. Share those memories with Jesus or your higher power, and let yourself be cared for in any way that you wish. Breathe deeply and let that care fill the places within you that need it the most.

6

The Distractor Sadducee

The Jews of a small town in Russia were eagerly awaiting the arrival of a Rabbi. This was going to be a rare event, so they spent a lot of time preparing the questions they were going to put to the holy man. When he finally arrived and they met with him in the town hall, he could sense the tension in the atmosphere as all prepared to listen to the answers he had for them.

He said nothing at first; he just gazed into their eyes, and hummed a haunting melody. Soon everyone began to hum. He started to sing and they sang along with him. He swayed and danced in solemn, measured steps. The congregation followed suit. Soon they became so involved in the dance, so absorbed in its movements that they were lost to everything else on earth; so every person in that crowd was made whole, was healed from the inner fragmentation that keeps us from the Truth.

It was nearly an hour before the dance slowed down and came to a halt. With the tension drained out of their inner being, everyone sat in the silent peace that pervaded the room. Then the Rabbi spoke the only words he pronounced that evening: "I trust that I have answered your questions."[1]

The Distractor Child

This Jewish rabbi is a healthy version of the fun-loving child, because he knows that answers to life's questions can be found in celebrating the present moment. Family therapists also refer to this child as the clown, mascot, family pet, entertainer, distractor, etc. He or she is the opposite of the fearful, introverted lost child. When unhealthy, this extroverted child buries fear and shame by moving toward people and getting positive attention. When breaking a cup, this child tries to joke about being clumsy and then seeks friends for comfort. He or she often appears as the happiest child in the family but may actually be using humor and laughter to cover pain. When others get upset, this child shrugs and says, "What's the big deal?" Thus the fun loving child is also called the "distractor," because he or she tries to distract the family from the pain of real problems, such as alcoholism, etc.

This child is addicted to bringing relief to the family through humor. Of all the types, the distractor has the most acquaintances (but few real, intimate friends), charms everyone and can usually get its way. This child is frequently the youngest, who got lots of attention for being cute. Even if not the youngest, this child may act younger than its age, loves the spotlight and got it at home. Almost all the anchorpersons on TV are the youngest child in their families.

I (Matt) have a little of the fun-loving distractor in me, although most got stamped out by my serious, responsible Pharisee. As a child, I loved to make people laugh. I frequented joke shops to buy car-exhaust whistles for the groom's car and a farting cushion to be placed strategically where deaf, eighty-year-old Uncle Harry would sit and wonder why everyone was looking at him. We had a plate palpitator that made his plate bounce every time he tried to put his peas on his fork. A hidden suction cup kept his saucer stuck to his cup. He drank from a glass with a hole and his ice cube had a plastic bug. These were my ways of getting even with Uncle Harry for always being so cold and wanting the heat turned up to 84 while we spent a scintillating evening discussing his aches and pains. I covered my frustration with Uncle Harry by laughing it away.

The Sadducee: Embrace the World & Keep the System Going

Unlike the Essenes, the Sadducees did not fear the world but unquestioningly embraced it. Their motto was "keep Rome happy at all costs." The Roman occupation aligned itself with the wealthy Sadducee aristocrats and priests. Rome allowed them to continue to dominate the Sanhedrin that governed their fellow Jews. In return for the power they received from Rome, the Sadducees promised to keep their fellow Jews under control. Thus the Sadducees kept trying to distract the Jews with "privileges" so that they wouldn't rebel and notice how much they were oppressed. "Just think how lucky you are to still have a temple," kept a Jew from thinking twice about rebelling against Rome and losing the temple too. The temple became the headquarters for maintaining the Sadducees' privileged position and wealth, since they controlled temple worship and temple funds. Jesus challenged their wealth and merchandizing practices (e.g., doves approved for sacrifice cost fifteen times more when they were sold in the temple) when he cleansed the temple (Jn 2:19). To justify their privileged position, the Sadducees selectively read the scriptures. For instance, they accepted the Pentateuch (first five books of the Old Testament) but rejected the prophets or anything that would challenge the status quo. That is why the Sadducees (the Sanhedrin and Caiaphas) wanted to sentence Jesus to death for supposedly claiming that he, and not Rome, was king and that he would destroy their corrupt temple (Mt 26:57–62, Lk 23:1).

A friend shared with us a contemporary example of keeping the system going at all costs, as the Sadducees did for the Romans. Our friend, a priest, was making a video series on moral issues in the Church. Everything had to be approved by his bishop. When they came to the section on birth control, our friend wanted to say on camera that this is a controversial issue in the Catholic Church. The bishop said, "No. You can't say that." Our friend said, "But it *is* a highly controversial issue. Everyone in the Church knows that." The bishop answered, "But you can't say it. We don't want people to think we're divided." Our friend said, "But we are." The bishop insisted, "But we can't let people know that." Sadducees, distractor children and sometimes good Christians keep the system going by smiling, accommodating, and pretending all is well.

Sadducees and distractor children may use religion addictively by losing themselves in its celebrative side, in order to anesthetize pain. No matter how troubled they feel, they are tempted to bury their negative feelings by singing, praising God, or focusing on heaven where all will be well. They may spiritually abuse others by trying to pray away, praise away, or otherwise spiritually manipulate whatever negative feelings others may try to share. They may also use religion addictively to justify all their other addictive distractions. For example, they may tune in to television evangelists who tell them that prestige, power and material wealth are God's blessings (sure to be granted if you donate right now to the Linns' ministry . . .).

The Gift Side of the Sadducee

The Sadducee also has a positive side that I (Matt) lack and need. Like the child everyone dotes over, he (as far as we know, the Sadducees were all men) can easily experience that God, too, loves him unconditionally just as he is. He can find this loving God in all things and in other cultures, such as the Roman world. By accommodating himself to everything, the Sadducee has a universal (the root meaning of "catholic") love that accepts everything as it is rather than trying to change it. The Sadducee with his smiling God enjoys the present moment, in contrast to my dour Pharisee always trying harder. The Sadducee can smile because he rejects the Pharisee's 613 precepts of the law requiring purifications and fasting for all. The Sadducee loves wealth, Roman parties and a good time. He believes in a God of life.

As the serious, responsible child, I need the Sadducee's God. My Irish side is more ready to find God in fasting than in feasting. I look into a refrigerator and think of cleaning up leftovers rather than asking myself what would I really enjoy eating. I am more attracted to Jesus fasting in the desert than inviting himself out for a five star meal with Zacchaeus. I surely would have taken Mary Magdalene's expensive ointment and sold it for the poor instead of having it wasted on my feet.

The ideal is St. Francis of Assisi, who can enjoy and celebrate all of creation, while his body bears the stigmata of the cross. He dances naked in joy over giving away all his clothes, and yet possesses all of creation as he embraces Brother Wolf and sings the Canticle of the Sun. When there is no money to give a poor mother who comes begging, Francis tells his brothers to sell the valuable, hand-copied scriptures. Unlike the religious addict, Francis knew it is better to live by the scriptures and care for the poor than to possess the scriptures and not live them.

Discovering the Root Negative Memories

What hurts can create a pattern of either avoiding pain by seeking enjoyable distraction, or the other extreme of avoiding anything enjoyable? Erikson points out that between the ages of three and five, our task is to learn how to play and enjoy new experiences. This lays the foundation for the capacity to take initiative. If we are hurt at this stage, then the playful, distractor child may be stamped out or may compulsively act out to avoid shame and guilt.[2]

During this stage my parents encouraged me to play some sport outside everyday. But since I was told each day to get out and play, it became a duty to go over to the playground. There I stood around until I was the last one chosen, again because I was the shortest and slowest. I also recall going to scout camp for two weeks of play. I got lonesome and wanted to return. Instead, the counselors pushed me to play more. They made me paddle the canoes, practice casting and eat ice cream, to distract me from being lonely. It didn't work and I felt even lonelier because I was singled out for special treatment. Finally I wrote a letter home asking my dad to come 300 miles to pick me up. Two days later when a camp counselor was returning to Minneapolis, he offered to take me home. I thought I would arrive before my dad even got my letter. But when I got home, I found that he had driven up to camp to get me. I was ashamed of getting lonesome, having to go home, and having my dad drive 600 miles for nothing. I associated play with shame and failure, and with not being free to feel what I felt, think what I thought, and choose what I wanted.

Both my German and Irish roots also made it difficult to enjoy the present. My German father lived through the depression of the 1930's and he taught us, "A penny saved is a penny earned." We would go to the grocery store with a handful of coupons. We waited forever for big items to be on sale. I learned to always save and delay gratification. The Irish spirituality of "offer it up" also reinforced this. God loved pain and sacrifice and the more it hurt, the more it pleased God. For example, our Irish nuns had us give up candy during Lent and save the money. According to the nuns, every dollar saved ransomed a pagan baby. Those that weren't ransomed starved to death and went to hell because they weren't baptized. Even after Lent, when I got back to eating candy bars, with each bite I felt guilty for choosing candy rather than more pagan babies. I rationalized that I had to eat candy or it wouldn't be hard to give it up next Lent and therefore wouldn't merit anything. It sounds humorous now, but at the time it kept me from knowing that God celebrates when I enjoy good things.

Sexuality was another gift not to be enjoyed unless you wanted a big family. The nuns were always measuring the skirt length on my grade school classmates to see if it covered those sexy, knobby knees. I shouldn't blame these nuns because my sister had to wear a raincoat to enter St. Peter's in Rome when the Swiss Guard saw her sleeveless dress. (The same thing happened to Sheila at the Garden of Gethsemane.) When taking walks as Jesuit novices, we wore hot, black jackets to cover our hairy arms lest some love-starved maiden start chasing us. Jansenist spirituality, which emphasized human depravity, left us with a God who didn't like bodies.

Discovering Our Positive Healing Memories

Just as negative memories cripple us until surfaced and healed, positive memories empower us to open again to the life we experienced previously. I have many positive memories because my family encouraged play, and for the most part I enjoyed it. I especially enjoyed family vacations. Dennis and I spent each summer in the library reading up on where we might want to go. After we finally decided, for two weeks we led our family on a five or six thousand mile odyssey. We drove through all the national parks before they became crowded. Our favorite was the Grand Canyon, where we tried to spit a mile before Mom said we were too close to the edge. We also saw the Horn and Hardart automats in New York City where a kid could insert coins and be rewarded with a huge slice of coconut cream pie. I was going to grow up to own one, and then I could eat all ten kinds of pie all day long.

Friends have also helped me learn to enjoy life. I recall a recent trip with our friend, Jack McGinnis. We took our time going from Boston to Houston in a van filled with snacks and music. I knew what the rest of the trip was going to be like when we made three rest stops in the first ninety minutes, even though there was nothing to rest from. We were always stopping for ice cream or a Chinese feast. We went out of our way to visit friends and to swim in the Smoky Mountains. Jack is teaching me how to enjoy getting someplace even more than arriving. When he travels by plane, he brings four suitcases filled with a coffee maker, computer (on which he works a little and plays a lot of poker), his pillow, a teddy bear for his inner child, music tapes and whatever else he thinks he might need to enjoy himself. Last time he even brought his toaster and had a friend travel 800 miles to bring him home-made bread. In contrast, I travel with one carry-on bag. Jack is stretching me into enjoying the present moment rather than working hard for that perfect moment that forever vanishes into the future. I get healed by being with the people who have what I need. Who are the people who have what you need?

The Distractor Sadducee Can Be Healed by Having Fun

Healing doesn't have to be serious work but can be fun when you have a weak distractor-Sadducee who needs more play. On my thirty-day retreat several years ago, my director told me I was into my Pharisee, praying six hours a day and striving too hard to make the perfect retreat. He suggested that each day I take the afternoon to just enjoy life. I decided to play basketball at nearby Creighton University. But being 5'3" while everyone else was about 6'3", my first game was a disaster. They blocked all my shots. I never grabbed a rebound. Although I was forty, a part of me was still ten years old and feared that if I didn't play better, I would again be the last one chosen. I kept telling myself to try harder. The next game, while reaching for a rebound, I wrecked my glasses as I bumped into the knees of a giant. He grabbed my rebound before it was even in my eyesight. But this time I laughed. Eventually I learned to play for sheer enjoyment, something I never did as the shortest kid. This was healing for my serious inner child who had to be perfect.

My prayer became more alive as each afternoon I asked myself what I would enjoy. I then let God love me whether or not I missed another rebound, burnt a gourmet meal, or grew weeds instead of the world's largest pea pod. I risked trying new things, even though I knew I couldn't do them perfectly. For example, I learned welding and began welding nails into designs. Crosses were the easiest thing to make. I kept the first cross I welded with its many mistakes rather than the last, more perfect one. That first cross continues to remind me that I can be the Sadducee enjoying the present moment instead of the Pharisee striving for perfection.

As I gave my Sadducee permission to enjoy the present in a healthy way, he balanced my responsible Pharisee. Now they all want to have more fun! When my Pharisee gets too serious, my Sadducee quotes from the Pharisee's Talmud, "God will judge us for every good thing God gave us that we failed to enjoy."

HEALING PROCESS

1. When did you experience having fun and being loved deeply? Recall those memories and breathe in once again the life you experienced.

2. Is there something enjoyable that you could do with a friend or your higher power that would give you new life in a similar way?

7

Generational Healing
of Spiritual Abuse

Robert Bly relates the following story, told to him by the Hungarian architect, George Docsi:

> When I was a boy I loved dinner. I loved to go into the dining room and sit in front of the big plates, and have the maid come in and serve the soup. One evening I went downstairs, and the dining room was in an uproar. A pogrom had taken place in Russia, and many Jews were fleeing over the border into our town. My grandfather went down to the railway station and brought home Jews whom he found there. I didn't know what was going on, but I could see old men with skull caps in the living room, mothers nursing babies in the corners of the dining room, and I threw a fit. I said, "I want my supper! I want my supper!" One of the maids offered me a piece of bread. I threw it on the floor and screamed, "I want my supper!" My grandfather happened to enter the room at that moment and heard me. He bent down and picked up the piece of bread, kissed it, and gave it to me. And I ate it.

Commenting on this story, Robert Bly writes,

> Most fathers in such a scene are liable to get angry—I have done it so often with my children—and shout at the child and say, "Pick it up! Children are starving in Africa!" or some

idiocy of that sort. George's grandfather skipped that whole scene and himself bent down, yet the child in no way compelled that. Then the kissing of the bread is very beautiful, I'm not sure why. It doesn't accuse the bread of being wicked, or the child, and the act is spontaneous, decisive and full of true authority and genuine grief. George Docsi later said, "You know, I think there's a little of my grandfather in me now."[1]

We learn patterns of shame in our families, and these patterns did not begin with our parents. George Docsi learned from his grandfather not to shame children or Jews. Perhaps George's grandfather learned this from his own grandfather, who in turn may have learned it from a family line whose reverence for the dignity of all persons and all things was never contaminated by shame. Just as an attitude of reverence for oneself and for others is passed down from one generation to the next, so is shame.

I (Sheila) am primarily a lost child (with an overlay of responsible child which I acquired as the oldest in my family). I have spent much of my life handling shame by trying to become invisible. For example, in groups I have usually felt myself involuntarily contracting, as if I were trying to take up as little space as possible in order to hide. In such situations I have felt disconnected from my real self as well as from others. Although our work requires that I often speak to large groups, as soon as I leave the podium I can virtually disappear in the crowd, hardly to be seen again until the next time I have to speak.

How did I learn this "disappearing act"? At first glance it seems that my immediate family background could account for my choice of the lost child role. Because of my mother's mental illness, she was unaware of appropriate social behavior, such as table manners, personal hygiene and verbal courtesy. In public she frequently behaved in inappropriate ways that provoked rejection and ostracism from others. When I was with her in such situations, I felt immense shame and I wanted to disappear so that no one would know I was my mother's child. However, I've realized that my lost child role was created for me long before I was born.

Like George Docsi's dinner guests, my mother's family was driven out of Russia during a pogrom. They came to the United States in 1902. My father's family went from France to Poland, and then some of them emigrated to the United States in 1920. Only my father's immediate family came to the United States; the rest remained in Poland, in a small town near the Russian border. When the Nazis came, my ancestors hid in the forests . . . trying to disappear. Three of my father's cousins survived; all the rest were captured by the Nazis and killed.

My family associated their suffering with Christianity. For example, shortly after I became a Christian I went to visit my father's four sisters. Anne, the youngest and the aunt to whom I am closest, invited me to stay with her. She told me that my three other aunts would welcome me too, but they felt anxious about seeing me since I had become a Christian. Their immediate fear was that I would arrive in their homes wearing a cross. Then she told me what the cross symbolized for her three older sisters, who were born in Poland. Anne said that Easter Sunday was a holiday for the Polish soldiers. They celebrated by going out with bayonets to hunt Jews. As children, Anne's sisters spent Easter Sundays hiding in the basement from the Polish soldiers. For my aunts, the cross meant terror rather than resurrection. They too learned to hide.

Healing Ancestral Hurts

Although I was not yet even born during World War II, throughout my adult life I have felt intense terror and grief whenever I encounter images of the holocaust. I cannot attribute this to experiences of anti-semitism. I grew up in largely Jewish neighborhoods in comfortable suburbs of the United States, and, unlike my aunts, I have no childhood memories of discrimination against Jews.

Why then am I so sensitive to suffering that I did not myself experience? I believe that the experiences of our ancestors, especially unresolved traumatic experiences such as religious persecution and spiritual abuse, are passed on to us in some mysterious way that we do not yet understand. Researchers studying memory have speculated that the cells themselves have some form of memory and that these memories are stored in our bodies. Perhaps such memories affect the DNA itself. However ancestral hurts are stored, the three of us have often found it helpful to pray for generational healing, and we have written about this elsewhere. [2]

Recently a friend was praying with me for healing of my lost child pattern of disappearing in groups. I expected that I would get in touch with shame-filled childhood memories of my mother's inappropriate behavior. Instead, when I became still, I saw all around me an ocean of grieving, terrorized people shrouded in gray. I knew these were my ancestors who were driven out of Russia, hunted by Polish soldiers and then killed during the holocaust—all because they were Jews. For centuries they had been driven from one country to another, refugees who were literally lost. I understood for the first time how I have carried their grief and terror and why I have spent my life "hiding in the forest" . . . trying to disappear.

This ocean of people shrouded in gray covered all of Europe. They seemed immobilized, as if they were not free to move on into the next life. When I asked them what they needed, I sensed that they had lost all hope in the face of overwhelming evil. In order to go on, they needed to know that evil never ultimately wins. For me this is the fundamental message of Christianity: evil never wins, because Jesus overcame it on the cross through love. Evil cannot destroy the intrinsic goodness of any part of creation. I understand now why my journey of faith began with nature . . . in the forest. There I learned (practiced, as it were) to see the goodness in simple things like stones and blades of grass. I developed a habit of recognizing the intrinsic goodness of all things, a habit that predisposed me to appreciate the significance of Jesus' life and death. I can say to my ancestors, "Evil never wins. It has been overcome through love."

My entire process of embracing Christianity and my Christian life since then might be seen as healing the effects of religious persecution upon generations of my family. I shared in the first chapter how my decision to become a Christian took place in an environment of spiritual freedom. The symbol of this for me is Leo, the Dominican priest who told me:

> God loves Jewish people just the same as Christians. God will love you every bit as much if you never become a Christian.

I think Leo's words comforted not only me, but generations of my people who were shamed and even killed because they would not become Christians.

I invited that ocean of gray, shrouded people into a scene that has recurred in my prayer for many years. The scene is an ancient home in Jerusalem, overlooking the valley to the north. The home is made of the yellow stone that still characterizes the buildings in the old part of the city. It is a very simple home, like those in Jesus' time, and Jesus' family is there. The doorway faces north, and in it there is a rocking chair. Someone sits in the chair and rocks me— sometimes it is a man and sometimes a woman. This person rocks me with the utterly personal tenderness of God who is Mother and Father. The sun is setting, and the colors of the sunset seem to contain all the infinite and powerful creative life of God. As the personal tenderness of God and the powerful creativity of God intersect in that doorway, I feel that I am rocking across eternity.

One by one, I invited the gray people to take my place in the rocking chair. As each one was held and comforted, I said with Jesus,

> God loves Jewish people just the same as Christians. God will
> love you every bit as much if you never become a Christian.

And then I said,

> Evil never wins. It has been overcome through love.

Each one remained as long as he or she needed, absorbing love
until the gray shroud lifted off and the person was taken up into
the light of the sunset.

In the days that followed this prayer, I noticed that a gray
shroud seemed to have lifted off of me as well. To Denny's surprise, I accepted invitations to two social events that I normally
would have avoided. I am in a process of healing that is ongoing,
and groups are still not the most comfortable setting for me.
However, when I am in groups now I feel noticeably more con-
nected to others and to my real self. I often feel myself expanding
rather than contracting, as if I am taking up my rightful amount
of space in the room.

I became a lost child not only because of experiences in my
nuclear family, but also because of the spiritual abuse suffered by
generations of my ancestors. Perhaps other Jews carry our ancestral hurts by adopting different roles, such as the rebels who lead
the United States civil rights and other social justice movements,
the responsible children who fill the helping professions with a
disproportionate number of Jews, or the distractor Jewish enter-
tainers who populate Hollywood.[3]

Reconciliation Across Religious Barriers

It has always been important for me to integrate Judaism
and Christianity within myself, rather than choose between
them. Once I knew Jesus' name, I hesitated over whether to be

baptized. My hesitation had nothing to do with theology; rather, it came from a fear of betraying my ancestors who had suffered at the hands of Christians. One day I was praying in the local Newman Center chapel, and I noticed a statue of Mary in the corner. I told her my hesitation, and I seemed to hear her saying, "I was a Jewish girl too, and I still am." It was only then that I felt free to be baptized, knowing that I could carry within myself the process of reconciliation between Christianity and Judaism that is necessary to heal centuries of religious persecution. An obvious sign of this reconciliation is my marriage to Dennis and my friendship with Matt, both of whom (besides being Christians) are half German.

As we look around the world, the most severe and seemingly irreconcilable conflicts seem to be in places with long histories of religious persecution, such as Yugoslavia, the Middle East and Northern Ireland. We wonder if such conflicts can ever be resolved unless ancient hurts underlying them are healed.

As I receive healing for the ancient hurts in my family, I find myself strengthened to do whatever I can so that others will not suffer in the same way. I think it is no accident that I work in full-time ministry primarily in the Roman Catholic Church, with people whose ancestors killed my ancestors. If I were to identify a common theme underlying everything I teach and write, it would be a passionate insistence that no one's spiritual freedom ever be compromised in the name of religion. I think my insistence comes from an all too real awareness of how religion can be used to shame and coerce others. I am aware of expressing that insistence as we write this book. I think my life has prepared me to say to the Church that I dearly love:

> Don't do to your own people what you did to mine; don't kill them by taking away their freedom to think what they think, feel what they feel and find their own unique way to God.

Generational Healing by Reaching Out

Thus far in this chapter we have spoken of how healing the hurts of spiritual abuse suffered by our ancestors in the past can heal us and empower us to heal situations of abuse in the present. Another way to heal our generational wounds is to begin in the present, and reach out to a person who represents the spiritual abuse suffered by our ancestors.

Julie and Michael Weisser told us how they did this.[4] Michael is a cantor in a Jewish synagogue in Lincoln, Nebraska and Julie is a nurse. In 1991, they began receiving anti-Jewish hate mail from Larry Trapp, the Grand Dragon of the Nebraska Ku Klux Klan. Larry's purpose was to terrorize Michael, Julie and their children into leaving the community. In order to accomplish this he planned to bomb the Weissers' home. Michael called Larry and left messages on his answering machine, calmly but firmly confronting Larry's abuse. Knowing Larry was disabled, Michael ended one of his messages with:

> Larry, the very first laws that the Nazis passed were against people like yourself, who have physical disabilities, and you would have been among those to die under the Nazis. Why do you love the Nazis so much?

One day Larry answered the phone and began to shout at Michael. Michael knew Larry had a hard time getting around because of his disability, and asked if Larry would like a ride to the grocery store. Larry grew very quiet and said, "I've got that taken care of, but thanks for asking." A few months later, he called Michael and Julie and said, "I want to get out of this, but I don't know how." Michael and Julie brought dinner to Larry, who burst into tears when they arrived.

Four weeks later Larry was told that his illness was terminal. Michael and Julie invited Larry into their home and Julie quit her job so that she could give Larry the full-time nursing care he needed. She soon realized that Larry's most crippling illness was loneliness. He had been abused throughout his childhood and had no close family. Michael, Julie and their children adopted Larry into their family and gave him the childhood he never had, including his first birthday party.

Larry wanted to make amends to everyone he had hurt. He joined the NAACP and wrote letters to all the people he had harassed. When Michael's synagogue hosted an interfaith celebration of Martin Luther King's birthday, Larry came and publicly apologized for his racism.

Larry was from a Roman Catholic background, and Michael supported him in practicing his Christian faith. But Larry believed that Judaism had saved him, and he wanted to become a Jew. When Larry applied to join Michael's synagogue, some members of the congregation were hesitant to accept a man who had only recently been a Nazi and who to them represented generations of persecution. As they met to discuss Larry's application, Michael told them he could not continue to minister to them if Larry was not accepted. The turning point came when a holocaust survivor spoke on Larry's behalf. She said,

> If a synagogue can't be forgiving, where is there for this man
> to go? We must forgive him.

Deeply moved by the example of this woman whose own ancestors had been killed by the Nazis, the other synagogue members decided that if she could forgive Larry then they could too. They voted unanimously to accept Larry, who finally had what he wanted all of his life: a sense of belonging.

Larry died in September, 1992, nine months after he moved in with the Weissers. He died in the home he had terrorized, holding the hands of the people he had persecuted. Larry and the Weisser family had broken the chain of spiritual abuse, for themselves, for their ancestors, and for everyone who watched their friendship.

HEALING PROCESS

1. Think back over your family line and ask God to show you any places along the way where your ancestors were the victims or the perpetrators of spiritual abuse and religious persecution. Who was shamed and punished for what he or she believed? Who shamed or punished others for what they believed?

2. Imagine those people standing before you, and ask God what healing words he or she wants to say to them.

3. Breathe those words into yourself, and breathe them out into your mother's line and into your father's line. Let them heal any patterns of shame that have affected you and your family.

4. Is there any way you feel moved to reach out to an individual or a group that has persecuted or been persecuted by you or your ancestors?

Introduction to Chapters 8 & 9: What Does Jesus Say & What Would Jesus Do?

In Chapters 3–6, we explored four roles that children learn in order to handle shame. During our retreats, we sometimes ask participants how they would have responded as children to the shameful situation of breaking their mother's favorite cup. Their responses vary, depending on what role they learned in childhood. Yet most people agree about one thing: they would have told no one about the broken cup. The reason they usually give is fear of punishment, especially the physical punishment of being spanked or slapped by a parent. Physical punishment only reinforces the shame that a child already feels.

Parents often learn such shaming ways of relating to children from religious authorities. These authorities frequently use scripture to reinforce their abusive teachings. Alice Miller gives the following example of how scripture has been used to sanction shaming and cruel behavior toward children:

> "He who spares the rod hates his son, but he who loves him is diligent to discipline him," we read in Proverbs [13:24]. This so-called wisdom is still so widespread today that we can often hear: A slap given in love does a child no harm. . . . If people weren't accustomed to the biblical injunction from childhood, it would strike them as the untruth it is. Cruelty

is the opposite of love, and its traumatic effect, far from being reduced, is actually reinforced if it is presented as a sign of love.

. . . No one ever slaps a child out of love but rather because in similar situations, when one was defenseless, one was slapped and then compelled to interpret it as a sign of love. . . .

If a mother can make it clear to a child that at that particular moment when she slapped him, her love for him deserted her and she was dominated by other feelings that had nothing to do with the child, the child can keep a clear head, feel respected, and not be disoriented in his relationship to his mother.[1]

How do we know whether scriptural injunctions, such as Proverbs 13:24, are healthy or shaming? Chapters 8 and 9 will explore how we can use scripture and religion in a healthy, non-shaming way.

8

Scripture & Spiritual Abuse

The Commander of the Occupation troops said to the Mayor of the mountain village: "We are certain that you are hiding a traitor in your village. Unless you give him up to us, we shall harass you and your people by every means in our power."

The village was, indeed, hiding a man who seemed good and innocent and was loved by all. But what could the Mayor do now that the welfare of the whole village was threatened? Days of discussions in the Village Council led to no conclusion. So the Mayor finally took the matter up with the village priest. The priest and the Mayor spent a whole night searching the Scriptures and finally came up with a solution. There was a text that said, "It is better that one man die and the nation be saved."

So the Mayor handed over the innocent man to the Occupation Forces, begging to be pardoned. The man said there was nothing to pardon. He would not want to put the village in jeopardy. He was tortured cruelly till his screams could be heard by all the village and finally he was put to death.

Twenty years later a prophet passed by that village, went right up to the Mayor and said to him: "What did you do? That man was appointed by God to be the saviour of this country. And you gave him up to be tortured and killed."

115

> *"What could I do?" pleaded the Mayor. "The priest and I looked at the Scriptures and acted accordingly."*
> *"That was your mistake," said the prophet. "You looked at the Scriptures. You should have also looked into his eyes."[1]*

Reading Scripture with Blinded Eyes

We all have blinders. For example, the Pauline author wrote,

> Slaves, be obedient to those who are your earthly masters, with fear and trembling, in singleness of heart, as to Christ . . . (Eph 6:5 RSV).

Paul did not tell slaves to become free, but rather to be just as subject to their masters as they would be to Christ. This was appealing to many, including Church councils. Until our present century they quoted this scripture passage to prove that their slaves were part of God's plan.[2] Reading scripture with blinders has contributed to many other abuses, such as the consignment of all Jews to hell at the Council of Florence in 1442, and the imprisonment of Galileo. The inquisition was based on John 15:6, "Anyone who does not remain in me will be thrown out like a branch and wither; people will gather them and throw them into a fire and they will be burned."

In our time, since the 1920's when women gained the right to vote, we are discovering our cultural blinders that have interpreted scripture to keep women subject to men. "Wives should be subordinate to their husbands as to the Lord" (Eph 5:22) was often quoted at weddings. We seldom preached on the previous verse of mutual submission, "Be subordinate to one another out of reverence to Christ." Too often we read scripture with eyes that see only what our culture accepts.

Scripture is still often interpreted in ways that are abusive to women. For example, "If anyone wishes to come after me, he must deny himself, take up his cross daily, and follow me" (Lk 9:23) is often used to support the idea that our greatest sin is a prideful refusal to surrender ourselves. However, as Ann Ulanov points out, "for a woman sin is not pride, the exaltation of self, but a refusal to claim the self God has given."[3] Developmentally, if a woman (or a man) has not yet been affirmed in her right to claim and assert herself, she should not be pressured to deny the self she does not yet possess. In our culture women are taught to be codependent, i.e., to deny their reality and their needs, and scripture has often been used to reinforce this.

Besides cultural blinders, we have blinders that come from Church doctrine. Two of us (Dennis and Matt) grew up in a Vatican I Church where we never questioned institutional authority. Even today, when someone asks us what the Church thinks about a given issue, we are likely to respond with what the Pope or hierarchy think. That's because, as Matthew 16 says, we are to submit to Peter's successors who have the "power of the keys."

> And I tell you, you are *Peter*, and on this rock I will build my church, and the powers of death shall not prevail against it. I will give *you* (singular) the *keys* of the kingdom of heaven, *and whatever you bind on earth shall be bound in heaven, and whatever you loose on earth shall be loosed in heaven* (Mt 16:19 RSV; italics ours).

As Matthew 16:19 clearly states, the "power of the keys" given to Peter means that "whatever you bind on earth shall be bound in heaven, and whatever you loose on earth shall be loosed in heaven." But we were never taught that this exact description of the "power of the keys" spoken to Peter in Matthew 16 is spoken to the entire people of God in Matthew 18. Thus the authority that previously was given only to Peter is now also given to "you" plural, to all the disciples, to the entire people of God.[4]

> Truly, I say to *you* (plural), *whatever you bind on earth shall be bound in heaven, and whatever you loose on earth shall be loosed in heaven* (Mt 18:17–18 RSV; italics ours).

Vatican II understood that Matthew 16 must be balanced by Matthew 18. Thus it defined "Church" not as previously defined by Vatican I to mean mainly the pope or the hierarchy, but rather as the entire "people of God." Vatican II made many changes to emphasize how the Spirit speaks not just to the hierarchy but also to the entire people of God. For instance, the change from Latin to the vernacular in liturgy ensured that everyone, and not just the hierarchy or priest who understood Latin, could communicate with the Spirit. Just how much Vatican II tried to remove our cultural blinders is indicated by the fact that it was the first council to say that the Spirit speaks through every culture and religion, not just our own.

Besides cultural and church blinders, we have a third, personal set of blinders, those that come from our hurts. When we were hurt, we probably felt inadequate and full of shame. The more we were hurt, the more we may have experienced, "Don't trust, don't talk, don't think, don't feel." Such messages taught us not to trust our own reality. If we distrust our own reality, it may be especially difficult for us to question that which is presented to us in the name of God, such as certain interpretations of scripture. We are afraid that if we question, we will be shamed and hurt again.

Religion is itself a way of handling the shame of hurts. The old saying, "There is no atheist in a foxhole," underlines how we instinctively turn to God when we feel hurt and powerless rather than in control. Therefore it is in the area of religion that we especially return to the shame patterns we learned when we felt powerless and out of control. As we have seen, our childhood patterns of handling shame (responsible child, rebel, lost child, distractor child) are often the same ways we handle shame when relating to the Church or to God.

We will therefore often read scripture with eyes blinded by our childhood patterns of handling shame. As a responsible child, Matt heard, "If you wish to be perfect, go, sell what you have . . . and come follow me" (Mt 19:21) and, thinking priesthood was the most perfect calling, became a Jesuit. Sheila, who was primarily a withdrawn lost child, might have read the same passage and withdrawn even further in despair that she could ever be perfect. A rebel might join a radical social justice group. The distractor might ignore the passage altogether or hope he can get a share of the treasures the responsible child is leaving behind.

These four compulsive patterns of responding to scripture come from shame that in turn comes from abuse. The most tragic part of abuse is that we tend to return to our abuser.[5] You may remember the story of Lisa Steinberg, the young girl who a few years ago was beaten to death by her father in New York City. Earlier that same evening Lisa had pleaded to go along with her father, who was on his way to a restaurant. She wanted to be with the only father she had, even though he habitually beat her. Lisa's behavior is typical of victims of abuse. For example, children of alcoholics frequently grow up to marry alcoholics. Such abuse victims recreate abusive situations about which they have unresolved feelings, in hopes of finally resolving those feelings. Moreover, when we are abused, one of the feelings we have is shame. In our shame we feel that all we deserve is more abuse, which leads to even more shame.

Just as we may return to abusive parents or others who resemble them, we may also return to an abusive image of God. Often at our retreats we speak about healing our image of God and mention that according to Catholic theology, God does not vengefully punish us by sending us to hell.[a] After this talk, sometimes a person will come up and angrily insist that "God does so send people to hell and if they're bad, they deserve it!" When we've been able to learn a little about such people's backgrounds, we've usually discovered that they were raised by harsh parents who severely punished them. These people seem to be fighting for an image of God as abusive and shaming as their own parents.

We can use scripture to reinforce an abusive image of God. If we feel shame before God, we will read the scriptures in a way that encourages us to feel even more worthless and worthy of even more rejection by God. Following are examples of how shame-based patterns learned in childhood, church teaching and cultural values can blind us as we read scripture.

Reading Scripture with Blinders of Shame

Remember the story of the woman who as a public sinner scandalizes Simon the Pharisee by washing Jesus' feet with her tears and drying them with her hair (Lk 7:36–50)? Jesus defends her with a sentence that is translated two different ways. See if you can pick the correct translation.

> For this reason I tell you that her sins, her many sins, must have been forgiven her, or she would not have shown such great love. It is the man who is forgiven little who shows little love (Lk 7:47, Jerusalem Bible).

---

a) The idea that God might punish us by sending us to hell is often such a basic factor in a shame-based relationship with God that we have written extensively about this elsewhere. See, for example, Dennis, Sheila & Matthew Linn, *Good Goats: Healing Our Image of God* (Mahwah, NJ: Paulist Press, 1994).[6]

or

I tell you that is why her many sins are forgiven—because of
her great love. Little is forgiven the one whose love is small
(Lk 7:47, New American Bible).

Which is right? The Jerusalem Bible stresses that love flows
out of prior *unearned* forgiveness whereas the NAB version emphasizes that love and repentance *earn* forgiveness. The answer to
which translation is correct comes from Jesus' question to Simon
in Luke 7:42, about whether the one forgiven a debt of five
hundred or one forgiven a debt of fifty will love more. Simon's
answer, that the one forgiven five hundred will love more, emphasizes that love flows from unearned forgiveness as a response
(Jerusalem Bible), rather than from a perfectionistic striving to
earn forgiveness.[7] Because nearly every Bible mistranslates this,
the Jerusalem Bible adds a footnote.

> Not as usually translated, 'her many sins are forgiven her
> *because* she has shown such great love.' The context de-
> mands the reverse: she shows so much affection because she
> has had so many sins forgiven.

The revised (1988) translation of the NAB agrees with the Jerusalem and now translates this passage in a similar way.

The fact that this passage is so frequently mistranslated may
be a sign of how much we believe that God acts on the American
ethic of "no free lunch," and that we have to work hard and *earn*
whatever we get. It may also be a sign of how shame-based most
of us are. Few of us know that we are loved and forgiven unconditionally, whether we love and forgive others or not. We read this
passage with eyes blinded by shame.

In fact, this is a story of stopping abuse and healing the roots
of shame. If the woman "had a bad name in the town," it was
probably from prostitution, especially since the Pharisees object

to how she kisses Jesus' feet. We know from studies that most prostitutes have been abused, and they subconsciously continue to seek abuse in prostitution. Furthermore, the Pharisees are presently abusing and shaming her with their judgmental stares, ignoring how she is coming with loving tears.

Abuse is healed when another stands with the one who has been abused as an "enlightened witness," and validates her or his reality.[8] That is exactly what Jesus does. Jesus validates the tearful woman and protects her from further abuse. For example, when she kisses Jesus' feet, the Pharisees misjudge her as propositioning Jesus. But Jesus defends her behavior as a sign of great love. With Jesus to love and affirm her as she is, the woman no longer needs to feel ashamed.

Reading Scripture with Church Blinders

If we are shame-based and afraid to question, we may read the scriptures with our Church's blinders. For example, Dennis and Matt grew up in the Vatican I Catholic Church that considered the religious life of contemplation as the most perfect way of life. Religious were holier than laity.[b] This theology rested on scripture passages, especially the story of busy Martha and prayerful Mary who chose the better part.

> Now as they went on their way, he entered a village; and a woman named Martha received him into her house. And she had a sister called Mary, who sat at the Lord's feet and listened to his teaching. But Martha was distracted with

---

b) Even the use of the words "laity" (which means the common or ordinary people) and "religious" betrayed the Church's bias. The implication was that some people were more (or less) ordinary than others, and that some were more (or less) religious than others.[9]

much serving; and she went to him and said, "Lord, do you not care that my sister has left me to serve alone? Tell her then to help me." But the Lord answered her, "Martha, Martha, you are anxious and troubled about many things; one thing is needful. Mary has chosen the good portion, which shall not be taken away from her" (Lk 10:38–42, RSV).

"Mary has chosen the good portion" was interpreted to mean that religious life was a higher calling, because its priority was to contemplate as Mary did. But this ignores the context. The story of Martha and Mary follows Jesus praising the lawyer for pointing out the great commandment of loving God and neighbor as yourself (Lk 10:25–28). Thus the focus is on love and not on action vs. contemplation. The next story is that of the Good Samaritan (Lk 10:29–37). This story stresses the layperson's loving action as superior to the behavior of the religious (the priest and the levite). Thus, the point is not whether we are lay or religious, nor whether we are active or contemplative. The point is whether we are experiencing love or anxiety. Are we "anxious and troubled about many things" (whatever our state in life, and whether we are praying or working) as was Martha, or are we giving and receiving deeper love as was Mary?

Reading Scripture with Cultural Blinders

Just as childhood patterns of shame and Church teaching can distort our reading of scripture, so can cultural values. As you read the following story, you might ask yourself who is the hero.

As they heard these things, he proceeded to tell a parable because he was near to Jerusalem, and because they supposed that the kingdom of God was to appear immediately. He said therefore, "A nobleman went into a far country to receive a kingdom and then return. Calling ten of his servants, he gave them ten pounds, and said to them, 'Trade with these till I come.' But his citizens hated him and sent an embassy after him, saying, 'We do not want this man to reign over us.' When he returned, having received the kingdom, he commanded these servants, to whom he had given the money, to be called to him, that he might know what they had gained by trading. The first came before him saying, 'Lord, your pound has made ten pounds more.' And he said to him, 'Well done, good servant! Because you have been faithful in a very little, you shall have authority over ten cities.' And the second came saying, 'Lord, your pound has made five pounds.' And he said to him, 'And you are to be over five cities.' Then another came, saying, 'Lord, here is your pound, which I kept laid away in a napkin; for I was afraid of you, because you are a severe man; you take up what you did not lay down and reap what you did not sow.' He said to him, 'I will condemn you out of your own mouth, you wicked servant! You knew that I was a severe man, taking up what I did not lay down and reaping what I did not sow? Why then did you not put my money into the bank, and at my coming I should have collected it with interest?' And he said to those who stood by, 'Take the pound from him and give it to him who has the ten pounds.' (And they said to him, 'Lord, he has ten pounds!') I tell you, that to every one who has will more be given; but from him who has not, even what he has will be taken away. But as for these enemies of mine, who did not want me to reign over them, bring them here and slay them before me" (Lk 19:11–27, RSV).

Whenever we have heard a sermon on this passage (or the similar talent parable in Matthew 25:14–30), the emphasis has been on using our gifts or talents well. The hero in such sermons is the servant who takes one pound and gets ten pounds and ten cities. God will reward us, too, if we take risks to serve God generously, and God will punish us if we hide our gifts. We end up feeling ashamed that we are not using our gifts well enough and afraid we will be punished. Thus, our cultural values of hard work, earn your own way, the poor are just lazy, and wealth is God's blessing get projected onto God.

In church we close this gospel passage with "The Good News of the Lord." But is this good news? The harsh king and the slaying of enemies seem like abuse rather than good news. This abusive behavior is our clue that the king probably does not represent God. In fact, there is evidence that the king was the Judean ethnarch, Archelaus. The Jerusalem Bible footnote says:

> Probably alluding to the journey of Archelaus to Rome in 4 B.C. to have the will of Herod the Great confirmed in his favor. A deputation of Jews followed him there to thwart the attempt.

On his return from Rome, the hated Archelaus put to death the fifty Jews who tried to block him from being confirmed as king. (Even Mary and Joseph, as they returned from Egypt, were warned in a dream in Matthew 2:22 not to return to Archelaus' Judean territory.) The hero then seems to be the man who keeps Archelaus' pound rather than investing it to earn more money to support Archelaus' tyranny. The others all become part of the ethnarch's repressive government as they receive cities to oversee. Archelaus committed so many atrocities that in 6 AD Caesar Augustus deposed him for fear the Jews would riot. Thus, if this interpretation is correct, the parable is really saying that we are to stand up and resist an abusive system at all costs.[10] (Perhaps that's why it follows the story of Zacchaeus, who renounces using the government tax system for abusive monetary gain.)

Jesus tells this parable on his way to Jerusalem and his passion. Like the parable's just servant, Jesus is sentenced to death because he has constantly resisted the abusive system by eating with sinners, healing on the sabbath, touching lepers, talking with a Samaritan woman, etc. As a resister, he is charged with wanting to destroy the temple system in three days and calling himself a king. The parable seems to be saying that if we confront an abusive system, like the just servant and Jesus himself, we will risk the cross. As others have followed in Jesus' footsteps, they have suffered persecution for releasing slaves from masters, supporting women's rights, and affirming the rights of the laity to be church.

Reading Scripture with Healed Eyes

How do we know when a certain interpretation of scripture should be challenged, or when one interpretation (e.g., the king as Archelaus) is more valid than another (e.g., the king as God)? A test to discover whether we are properly understanding a scripture passage (or a private revelation such as those given at Fatima or Medjugorje) is to judge our interpretation by its fruits. Since the most important fruit is love, we can ask ourselves, "When someone who loves me is loving me the most, would he or she act in this way?" And, since every authentic aspect of Christianity is good news, we can also ask ourselves, "Is it good news?" If the answers to these questions are "Yes," we probably understand the passage. If not, we are probably making a mistake, such as reading scripture with blinders or interpreting something literally which is really intended as an image.[c] In other words, scripture must leave the reader feeling loved rather than shamed.

---

c) This points to another reason why scripture is so commonly misused in abusive ways. The shame-based religious addict and religious abuser, who feel out of control internally, seek outer control through a rigid religious belief system. One means of such control is literalistic, black and white "letter of the law" thinking. Bill Wilson (co-founder of Alcoholics Anonymous) observed this kind of thinking in alcoholics, and family therapists identify it as characteristic of the dysfunctional families in which addicts are raised.

What we have done in looking for interpretations that are loving rather than shaming is what the authors of scripture themselves do. A common scripture verse for making ourselves feel unworthy is Matthew 5:48: "You must therefore be perfect just as your heavenly Father is perfect" (JB). Perhaps Luke sees this as a shaming statement tempting us to perfectionism, because he changes it to: "Be compassionate as your Father is compassionate" (Lk 6:36, JB). Thus Luke reinterprets Matthew's source and says that the only way we are to be like God is in extending God's merciful compassion to ourselves and others. Perhaps Luke learned to reinterpret scripture from Jesus, who was constantly reinterpreting scripture to follow the greater law of love (Mt 22:34–40). For example, Jesus reinterprets "An eye for an eye and a tooth for a tooth" (Ex 21:24):

> You have learnt how it was said: Eye for eye and tooth for tooth. But I say this to you: offer the wicked man no resistance. On the contrary, if anyone hits you on the right cheek, offer him the other as well . . . (Mt 5:38–39, JB).

Here Jesus is taking an unloving law of vengeance which comes from abuse and leads to further abuse. Jesus reinterprets it accord-

---

Thus, precisely because it is a concrete, written document, the Bible easily lends itself to misuse by religious addicts. Because they tend to take everything literalistically, religious addicts can easily mistake what is non-essential in the Bible for what is essential to the gospel. This is what happens in "proof-texting," in which individual passages are used to prove points that may not be consistent with the overall message of scripture (such as the use of John 15:6 to justify the inquisition). Since the Bible is a big book, full of pronouncements about all sorts of things, it is a "set-up" for misuse by literal-minded religious addicts and spiritual abusers. St, Paul was aware of this danger when he wrote, "God is the one who has given us . . . this new covenant, which is not a covenant of written letters but of the Spirit: the written letters bring death but the Spirit gives life" (2 Cor 3:6, JB). [11]

ing to the higher law of love. He continually sets aside laws such as those forbidding works of healing on the sabbath (Dt 5:12–15, Mt 12:9–14) when they are abusive rather than loving. If we don't interpret scripture as good news that empowers us to be loving rather than filled with shame, then we are following neither Jesus nor the authors of scripture who wrote after him.

Our friends Steve and Susan are raising their children to interpret scripture as good news. Steve and Susan have little extra money, and they had saved for a long time to buy nine-year-old Mark his first bicycle. One evening the new bicycle was stolen. Mark was heartbroken. Every morning at breakfast, Steve and Susan and their three children read the gospel for the day together and each one shares what he or she hears God saying. The morning after the bicycle was stolen, this was the gospel for the day:

> Love your enemies, do good to those who hate you, bless those who curse you, pray for those who treat you badly. To the man who slaps you on one cheek, present the other cheek too; to the man who takes your cloak from you, do not refuse your tunic. Give to everyone who asks you, and do not ask for your property back from the man who robs you (Lk 6:27–30, JB).

Upon hearing this, Mark turned red with anger and blurted out, "I've heard that reading before and I always knew I hated it!" His brother and sister, who understood Mark's pain about his stolen bicycle, expressed similar feelings. Steve and Susan encouraged the children to express their outrage at what Jesus seemed to be saying, that Mark should not try to recover his stolen bicycle. When all the angry feelings were out, Steve and Susan suggested that after dinner that evening the family gather together and study the Bible commentaries to see if they could understand what Jesus was really saying.

As they studied together and read the parallel passage in

Matthew 5:38–48, they learned that Luke 6:27–30 must be understood in the context of Jesus' effort to substitute love for the vengeance of "an eye for an eye" (Mt 5:38). The passage from Exodus that says "An eye for an eye and a tooth for a tooth" (Ex 21:24) had actually been a step in that direction for the Old Testament writers. They were trying to improve on the tribal custom of vengefully punishing an offender. Thus "An eye for an eye and a tooth for a tooth" means, "If an eye was taken from you, you can take *only* an eye back—not more." In this passage from Luke, Jesus is going one step further and saying, "No matter what another does to you, do not lose sight of his or her underlying value as a person." Jesus' point was not that we should let ourselves be robbed, but rather that an attitude of love is more important than stolen property. At the end of the evening, Mark said he thought he knew now what Jesus wanted to say to him:

> Jesus is saying that it's ok for me to try to find my bike. If I find the guy who took it, I'm going to ask him to give it back. But I'm not going to punch his lights out. I'm going to remember that Jesus loves him, even if I'm mad at him.

Steve and Susan are creating for their children an environment of spiritual health. Rather than shaming Mark for his angry reaction to the passage from Luke, his parents encouraged him to feel what he felt. Mark did not have to give up his reality and neither did he have to throw out the scripture. Steve and Susan supported Mark in exploring Jesus' meaning until he could understand it in a way that was good news. Because he is being raised in his family to feel what he feels and think what he thinks, Mark will not be vulnerable to spiritual abuse in his church.

When we read scripture and feel ashamed of our feelings, our desires, our call in life, or any other aspect of our real self, then we are reading it with blinders of spiritual abuse. We need to stop and question what we are reading and how it is being interpreted to us. Scripture may challenge us and it may call us to conversion, but it is not intended to shame us. Everything in scripture and everything in Christianity is meant to be good news. If anything isn't good news, then something is wrong and we have the right to keep searching until it becomes good news.

HEALING PROCESS

1. Take a scripture passage that you have wondered about or struggled with and try reading it as a responsible child, rebel, lost child, and finally as a distractor child.

2. Which one was easiest?

3. Is there anything in the passage that is not good news for you? How do you feel as you read that part of the passage? Take a moment to honor your feelings.

4. Ask God to help you understand this passage in a way that *is* good news for you. You may wish to read what comes before and after this passage to see if that helps you understand its context. It might be helpful to look up the parallel and related passages mentioned in your Bible. You may even want to study Bible commentaries on this passage. If none of this helps, you may wish to temporarily set aside this passage, giving yourself permission to wait until you can understand it in a way that is good news for you.

9

What Would Jesus Do?

I (Dennis) find hope for healing of spiritual abuse in the way my father and I worked through what could have been a very painful situation this past year. The way the situation was resolved is for me a model of how to protect ourselves from spiritual abuse. My father had just read a flier about a talk on "Healing Religious Addiction" that the three of us were going to give at a Franciscan retreat house. The flier said that often people who are over-controlled will escape through an addiction such as alcohol, sex, overeating or even religion. My father's response was, "If the priests and hierarchy had more control and people did what they were told, then we wouldn't have such things as alcohol, sex, or eating addictions." Looking me straight in the eye, he asked, "Are you going to be like C.J. Thies?"

As children, C.J. and Jenny Thies were like grandparents to Matt and myself. C.J. was a Protestant and Jenny a Catholic. C.J. would bring home pamphlets about the latest Catholic scandal, hoping that Jenny would read them and abandon the Catholic Church. Both Jenny and my father spent a lot of time figuring out how to dispose of those pamphlets so no one else would read them. Now my father feared that his own son would be another C.J. Thies, devoting his life to uncovering the latest Catholic scandal.

So I said to my father, "It must puzzle you a lot when we say that the Church can use power in a way that encourages addiction." My father repeated, "If people only did exactly as they were told by the Church, we'd have fewer problems." So I said, "Dad, do you remember what Joe Wright asked you while both of you were walking over to Mass?" (Joe Wright had visited my parents two years earlier and had told me this story.) My father responded, "Joe asked me if he could receive Communion." A very interesting question, once you know that Joe Wright is a Presbyterian pastor and my father is an eighty-year-old, German, Roman-to-the-core Catholic. The rest of the conversation between Dad and myself went as follows:

"Dad, how did you respond to Joe's question?"

"I told him to do whatever he believed was right."

"When you arrived at the church did you pick up a leaflet missal for both you and Joe?"

"Yes."

"And what does the Roman Catholic bishops' statement on the back of every leaflet missal say about Protestants receiving Communion?"

"It says that if you believe it's the body and blood of Christ, then you should receive."

"Dad, is that what the bishops' statement says?"

"Not exactly."

"What does it say?"

"It says that Communion is a sign of unity and that unless you are in union with Rome and the hierarchy, you should not receive."

"So why did you knowingly disobey what the bishops told you and allow a Protestant pastor to receive Communion with you?"

My father looked scared, as if being accused of "disobeying bishops" was worse than being accused of some great war crime. Finally, in total desperation, my father blurted out,

"I did what Jesus would have done!"

Eighty years had taught my father that only one rule is necessary: Do what Jesus would do. Canon law or any statement by the hierarchy is meant to be the Church's best attempt to say, "This is what we think Jesus would do." In fact, when a regulation does not seem to encourage what Jesus would do, then a person would err in obeying it. In not following the letter of the law but rather his own conscience, my father was aligning himself with a principle that is fundamental to Catholicism. Roman Catholic ethics has always affirmed the right to conscientiously object, insisting that a person must follow her or his own informed individual conscience, even when it conflicts with law.

What moved me was how my father had created an "informed conscience." In quoting to me the bishops' regulation, I knew he had respectfully considered what the bishops said. He had also respectfully considered what most Roman Catholic theologians and leaders involved in ecumenical dialogue would say, "If you believe it is the body and blood of Christ, then you can receive Communion." And finally, he knew the *sensus fidelium*, or what faithful people acting in good conscience would say. My father had attended various Catholic conferences with Joe, where Joe had asked other friends the same question. Almost always Joe had been given the same answer my father gave him. In short, my father had allowed the Church, defined by Vatican II as the entire "people of God," to inform his conscience.[a]

---

a) Part of the difficulty for my father in creating an informed conscience is that, with his Anglo-Saxon mindset, he was trying to interpret a Church law written with a Roman mindset. An example of these two distinct mindsets would be Sheila and myself. If I tell Sheila that we will leave at 8:30 PM, to my

Perhaps the best argument for my father's response to me is the Eucharist itself. Throughout the centuries as Christians have received Eucharist, the words have remained the same: "The body of Christ," to which the recipient responds, "Amen." St. Augustine reminded Communion recipients that "Amen" means "Yes, I am." In proclaiming "Amen," the recipient makes the most radical statement possible for a Christian, namely, "Yes, I am the body of Christ."

Even the name "Christian," which evolved from *alter Christus* (another Christ), declares, "Yes, I am the body of Christ." During the first centuries of the Church all Christians, and not just priests, were addressed as and understood their deepest identity to be that of *alter Christus*. Because our deepest identity is Christ (Gal 2:20), our response to canon law, to a Church authority or to any life situation reflects our true self to the extent we can say with my father, "I did what Jesus would have done."

HEALING PROCESS

In deciding how to respond to Joe, Dennis' father listened to his own life experience of healthy spirituality. All addiction, including religious addiction, comes from denial. Healing comes from telling the truth, first of all the truth about what is real within us. Any way in which we develop our ability to listen to our own life experience helps

---

Anglo-Saxon mind "8:30" means "8:30." But Sheila, who operates with a Roman mindset, thinks she is on time if she is ready to leave *around* 8:30, which could mean 9:00 (unless a person or a plane is waiting for us). Since Anglo-Saxon law means exactly what it says, its followers will often try to rigidly comply, e.g., not only putting it in the leaflet missal but even announcing the regulation during the liturgy. The bottom line of Roman law or Church law is not meant to be the letter of the law but rather the law my father relied on: What would Jesus do?

us develop a habit of telling the truth about what is real within us. Such a habit can protect us from religious addiction and the other effects of spiritual abuse.

One way that has helped many like ourselves is 12 Step groups, where each week we share our experience with a group of people who are committed to receiving it in a non-judgmental way that honors our reality. The honest sharing of other group members also increases our capacity to discover and tell the truth about what is real within us.

Another way that the three of us find helpful is a daily process of reflection on that day's experience. Each evening, we gather together and ask ourselves, "For what moment today was I most grateful and for what moment was I least grateful?" or, "When today did I most give and receive love and when did I least give and receive love?" After a few minutes of silence, each person shares his or her experience of that day.

Perhaps you would like to try this process alone or with another.

1. If so, put your feet flat on the floor, take a few deep breaths from the bottom of your toes, up through your legs, your abdominal muscles and your chest. Breathe out and bless all the space around you.

2. Place your hand on your heart and ask your higher power to bring to your heart the moment today for which you are most grateful. If you could relive one moment which one would it be? When were you most able to give and receive love today?

3. Share with your higher power exactly what was said and done in that moment that made it so special. Breathe in the gratitude you felt and receive life again from that moment.

4. Ask your higher power to bring to your heart the moment today for which you are least grateful. When were you least able to give and receive love?

5. Share with your higher power what happened in that moment that made it so difficult. Allow your higher power to be with you in whatever you feel without trying to change or fix it in any way.

6. Give thanks that you are an alive, feeling person. If possible, share as much as you wish of these two moments with a friend.

Reflection Questions for Group Sharing

CHAPTER 1

1. Who has provided healthy spiritual parenting for you, and how?
2. As you look back over your life, what experiences seem to you spiritually abusive? Is there any way in which you feel spiritually abused in your present life?
3. What has helped you to deal with these experiences of abuse?

CHAPTER 2

1. What are one or two of the most important ways that your image of God has changed since you were a child? Is there any way your image of God is in the process of changing now?
2. How has your religious experience affected your sexuality, positively or negatively?
3. Have you had any healing experiences with God the Mother?

CHAPTER 3

1. Do you have too much or too little of the responsible Pharisee?
2. What hurts might have led you to this pattern of handling shame?
3. What positive memories have helped heal this pattern?

CHAPTER 4

1. Do you want to be more or less of a rebel Samaritan?
2. Who is for you a model of a healthy rebel?
3. What has helped the gifts of the rebel grow in you?

CHAPTER 5

1. When have you been an unhealthy lost child? When have you been a healthy lost child able to use your intuitive and contemplative gifts?
2. What hurts or shaming situations contributed to the overdevelopment or underdevelopment of your lost child?
3. Is there anything you want to do to encourage your healthy lost child to grow?

CHAPTER 6

1. Who is a model for you of the gifted side of the distractor Sadducee, who celebrates life?
2. Do you tend more toward avoiding pain by seeking enjoyable distraction or toward avoiding enjoyment?
3. What events in your life might have shaped this behavior?

CHAPTER 7

1. Who in your family line were victims or perpetrators of spiritual abuse and religious persecution?
2. Can you identify any ways that you carry these generational wounds in your own life?
3. Is there any way you feel moved to reach out to an individual

or a group that has persecuted or been persecuted by you or your ancestors?

CHAPTER 8

1. What part of the chapter was most helpful to you in discovering a new way of interpreting scripture?
2. As you have struggled with your own cultural, Church, or personal blinders, is there a scripture passage you have come to understand in a new way?
3. What scriptural passage for you doesn't at first seem to be "good news"? Is there any way it could be read as "better news" so you feel loved rather than shamed by God as you read it?

CHAPTER 9

1. Can you recall a situation in which you felt empowered to act in a loving and courageous way because you knew that was what Jesus would do?
2. In what situation might you at times be acting differently than you think Jesus would act?
3. What national policies do we have that Jesus would not support? (For example, would Jesus ever use a nuclear bomb or condemn a criminal to death?)
4. What are we doing as a Church that Jesus would do differently?

Resources for Further Growth

BOOKS

Good Goats: Healing Our Image of God, by Dennis Linn, Sheila Fabricant Linn and Matthew Linn (Mahwah, NJ: Paulist Press, 1994). We become like the God we adore, and if our God is shaming and abusive we are likely to shame and abuse ourselves and/or others. One of the easiest ways to heal ourselves and our society is to heal our image of God, so that we know a God who loves us at least as much as those who love us the most. Discusses whether God throws us into hell or otherwise vengefully punishes us, and the role of free will. The main text is illustrated in full color, followed by a question and answer section that gives the theological and scriptural foundation for the main text.

Belonging: Bonds of Healing & Recovery, by Dennis Linn, Sheila Fabricant Linn and Matthew Linn (Mahwah, NJ: Paulist Press, 1993). Twelve-Step recovery from any compulsive pattern is integrated with contemporary spirituality and psychology. Defines addiction as rooted in abuse and as our best attempt to belong to ourselves, others, God and the universe, and helps the reader discover the genius underneath every addiction. Chapter 9 focuses on how a non-abusive image of God helps heal addictions.

Healing the Eight Stages of Life, by Matthew Linn, Sheila Fabricant & Dennis Linn (Mahwah, NJ: Paulist Press, 1988). Based on Erik Erikson's developmental system, this book helps to heal hurts and develop gifts at each stage of life, from conception through old age. Includes healing ways our image of God has been formed and deformed at each stage.

Healing of Memories, by Dennis & Matthew Linn (Mahwah, NJ: Paulist Press, 1974). A simple guide to inviting Jesus into our painful memories to help us forgive ourselves and others.

Healing Life's Hurts, by Dennis & Matthew Linn (Mahwah, NJ: Paulist Press, 1978). A more thorough book to help the reader move through hurts using the five stages of forgiveness.

Healing the Greatest Hurt, by Matthew & Dennis Linn and Sheila Fabricant (Mahwah, NJ: Paulist Press, 1985). Healing the deepest hurt most people experience, the loss of a loved one, through learning to give and receive love with the deceased through the Communion of Saints. Chapter 5 and Appendix A contain material on afterlife and the problem of hell.

These and other books by the authors are available from Paulist Press, 997 Macarthur Blvd., Mahwah, NJ 07430, (201) 825–7300.

TAPES & COURSES (FOR USE ALONE, WITH A COMPANION, OR WITH A GROUP)

Healing Our Image of God, by Dennis Linn, Sheila Fabricant & Matthew Linn (St. Louis: Christian Video Library, 1985). Set of two tapes which may be used to accompany this book and/or *Good Goats*.

Belonging: Healing & 12 Step Recovery, by Dennis, Sheila & Matthew Linn (Audio Version / Kansas City, MO: Credence

Cassettes, 1992). Audio or videotapes and a course guide to accompany book (see above), for use as a program of recovery.

Healing the Eight Stages of Life, by Matthew Linn, Sheila Fabricant & Dennis Linn (Mahwah, NJ: Paulist Press, 1985). Tapes
and a course guide which can be used with book (see above) as a
course in healing the life cycle. Available on videotape and in two
audio versions, condensed and expanded.

Prayer Course for Healing Life's Hurts, by Matthew & Dennis
Linn and Sheila Fabricant (Mahwah, NJ: Paulist Press, 1983).
Ways to pray for personal healing that integrate physical, emotional, spiritual and social dimensions. Book includes course
guide, and tapes are available in video and audio versions.

Praying with Another for Healing, by Dennis & Matthew Linn
and Sheila Fabricant (Mahwah, NJ: Paulist Press, 1984). Guide
to praying with another to heal hurts such as sexual abuse, depression, loss of a loved one, etc. Book includes course guide, and
tapes are available in video and audio versions. *Healing the Greatest Hurt* (see above) may be used as supplementary reading for the
last five of these sessions, which focus on healing of grief.

Dying to Live: Healing through Jesus' Seven Last Words, by Bill &
Jean Carr and Dennis & Matthew Linn (Mahwah, NJ: Paulist
Press, 1983). How the seven last words of Jesus empower us to fully
live the rest of our life. Tapes (available in video or audio versions)
may be used with the book *Healing the Dying,* by Mary Jane,
Dennis & Matthew Linn (Mahwah, NJ: Paulist Press, 1979).

Audio tapes for all of these courses (except *Belonging* and
Healing Our Image of God) are available from Paulist Press, 997
Macarthur Blvd., Mahwah, NJ 07430, (201)825–7300. *Belong-
ing* audio tapes are available from Credence Cassettes, 115 E.

Armour Blvd., Kansas City, MO 64111, (800)444–8910. *Healing Our Image of God* audio tapes are available from Christian Video Library, 3914-A Michigan Ave., St. Louis, MO 63118, (314) 865–0729.

Videotapes for all of these courses (except *Belonging*) may be purchased from Paulist Press. For information on *Belonging* videotapes, on *Good Goats: Healing Our Image of God* videotapes, and on videotapes to accompany this book, contact Christian Video Library at the above address and phone.

VIDEOTAPES ON A DONATION BASIS

To borrow any of the above videotapes, contact Christian Video Library.

SPANISH BOOKS & TAPES

Several of the above books and tapes are available in Spanish. For information, contact Christian Video Library.

RETREATS & CONFERENCES

For retreats and conferences by the authors on the material in this book and other topics, contact Dennis, Sheila & Matthew Linn, c/o Re-Member Ministries, 3914-A Michigan Ave., St. Louis, MO 63118, (314)865–0729.

Notes

INTRODUCTION

1. This story is based upon an experience related to us by Francis MacNutt.

CHAPTER 1: SPIRITUAL ABUSE & SPIRITUAL REPARENTING

1. Alice Walker, *The Color Purple* (New York: Simon & Schuster, 1982), 202–203.

2. Brian Swimme, Video series *Canticle to the Cosmos*, Program #1, "The Story of Our Time" (San Francisco: NewStory Project, 1990).

3. Martin Lang, *Acquiring Our Image of God* (Mahwah, NJ: Paulist Press, 1983), 20–21, 61, 100–101, 125–126.

Researchers in the field of psychology and religion have also found a correlation between the degree of positive bonding with parents and image of God. For example, in a study of 162 hospital patients, William Justice and Warren Lambert found that

> . . . those who have had strongly negative experiences with their parents (such as sexual abuse) tend to have a more negative concept of the personality of God: *those with the lowest image of their parents reported the lowest image of God.*

Of the 162 subjects, 14.9% reported sexual abuse by their parents, and every one of these 14.9% reported a substantially lower God image than those subjects whose parents were not sexually abusive. William G. Justice & Warren Lambert, "A Comparative Study of the Language People Use to Describe the Personalities of God and Their Earthly Parents," *The Journal of Pastoral Care*, 40:2 (June, 1986), 166–172.

Dr. Robert Stuckey, whose recovery units have treated over 20,000 addicts, confirms this connection between the quality of relationship with parents and the capacity for faith in God:

> People who have gone into A.A. with a very harsh view of God have a hard time. They have a harder time than the people who have had no religious training at all. Adolescents who have had no training about God are often the ones who end up with the warmest feelings about God. If they have no resentment for any authority figures, it flows easily from them. The more a person has a concept of God which is tied

in with authority figures that are resented, the harder it is for that person to have a direct new surge of energy which will help him overcome his addiction.

Dr. Robert Stuckey, M.D. "You Gotta Have Hope," *New Catholic World*, 232:1390 (July/August, 1989), 161.

A beautiful and intriguing counterpoint to these examples of how our relationship with God is affected by our parents is the work of Joan Fitzherbert. She suggests that just as small children are undifferentiated from their mother (or other primary caregiver) and in constant contact with her thoughts and feelings, so also they are in constant contact with the mind of God. The child may confuse these two " 'not-self' minds," so that "the picture of the idealized Good Mother may in fact be created in the image of God, and not vice versa." In other words, just as we may project our parents' personalities onto God, we may also project God's personality onto our parents. From our point of view, this means that children come here knowing God intimately, each in his or her own unique way. They do not need to have an awareness of God "poured into" them through religious training. Religious education should support and enhance this inner knowing rather than attempt to impose an externally defined way of knowing God. Joan Fitzherbert, "The Source of Man's 'Intimations of Immortality,' " *British Journal of Psychiatry*, 110 (1964), 859–862.

4. Ernest Kurtz, *Not-God: A History of Alcoholics Anonymous* (Center City, MN: Hazelden, 1991), 99.

5. Anne Wilson Schaef, "My Journey to Understanding Addictions," presentation at Fishnet Northeast Conference on "Recovering Intimacy and the Good News of the Gospel," June 24–28, 1990.

6. Peter McCall, O.F.M. Cap., has written an excellent brief article, "Religious Addiction and Abuse," in which he summarizes the characteristics of the addicted mind (denial, obsession,

compulsivity and grandiosity) as applied to religion (Dove Leaflet #32, available from Dove Publications, Pecos, NM 87552).

Because religious addiction functions within the personality just like any other addiction, the same Twelve-Step program that has helped so many alcoholics and other addicts can also help the religious addict. A support group was founded in 1985 for this purpose. For information, contact Fundamentalists Anonymous, P.O. Box 20324, Greeley Square Station, New York, NY 10001, (212)696–0420.

7. David Johnson and Jeff VanVonderen define religious addiction somewhat differently, as "The state of being dependent on a spiritually mood-altering system." Their definition sheds light on the fact that all of us tend to impose our own conversion experience upon others. In other words, we tend to perceive what will lead others (and ourselves in the future) toward God according to what we have previously experienced as leading us toward God. (In theologian Bernard Lonergan's terms, conversion precedes method.) It's as if our conversion experience gave us a "high," and we keep trying to recreate that high (and assume that others will get high in the same way). Cf. David Johnson & Jeff VanVonderen, *The Subtle Power of Spiritual Abuse* (Minneapolis: Bethany House, 1991), 190; Bernard J.F. Lonergan, S.J., *Method in Theology* (New York: Herder & Herder, 1972).

8. Bill Wilson, co-founder of Alcoholics Anonymous and author of its Twelve Steps, also understood this. Bill's own religious conversion experience was the source of his recovery from alcoholism, and in the early years of his work with other alcoholics Bill was greatly influenced by the Oxford Group religious revival movement. However, Bill eventually broke with the Oxford Group because of its emphasis on absolutes, i.e., beliefs that all members were required to hold. Bill realized that the shame-based dynamic of addiction is exacerbated rather than healed by the imposition of "shoulds" of any kind, especially religious shoulds.

Thus, while Bill regarded surrender to a higher power as essential for recovery, he took great care never to define that higher power for anyone else. For example, the phrase "God *as we understood Him*" occurs twice in the Twelve Steps, and alcoholics were encouraged to approach spiritual concepts by "honestly asking yourself what they mean to you." Bill had absolute confidence that if recovering people were in an environment of mutual commitment and honest sharing of experience, each person would find his or her own understanding of God. It seems to us that the remarkable success of the Twelve-Step recovery movement and its enduring spiritual vitality are a witness to the efforts of Bill and his followers to protect the movement against spiritual abuse.

Cf. *Alcoholics Anonymous*, Third Edition (New York: Alcoholics Anonymous World Services, 1976), Chapter Four, "We Agnostics." See also Dennis Linn, Sheila Fabricant Linn & Matthew Linn, *Belonging: Bonds of Healing & Recovery* (Mahwah: Paulist, 1993), especially the Preface and Chapter 9.

9. We are indebted to Maggie Scott Irwin, Director of Family Services at The Meadows Treatment Center in Wickenburg, Arizona, for our understanding of ritual abuse.

10. Karl Rahner says this in the context of writing on indifference as the first characteristic of Ignatian spirituality:

> By indifference is here meant an extremely alert, almost over-acute sense of the relativity of all that is not God himself. . . . Religious things included, for they too are not God. They too—that is, any particular exercises and methods, all the various devotions, practices, well-tried procedures and attitudes, all the established patterns in which the basic religious act of self-surrender to God gives itself concrete shape, and must do so if it is not to fade away into vagueness and dissipate into a vacuum—they are all included in this non-distinguishing indifference. They are all subject to this almost lethal law that everything other than God is provisional, subject to cancellation, liable to be other

than it is . . . otherwise tomorrow than what it is today. . . .
God is always greater than what we know of him, and greater
than the things which he himself has willed. His holy will,
that to which absolute allegiance is given, is never precisely
identical with anything willed by him. The particular thing
that is embraced as the realization of the will of God is always
subject to the proviso, penetrating to the very core of its
being, that this is "if, because, and so long as God pleases"
(Karl Rahner, *Mission & Grace*, Vol. III (New York: Sheed &
Ward, 1973), 181–183.

11. Personal conversation with Peter Campbell and Edwin
McMahon, Co-Directors, Institute for Bio-Spiritual Research,
Coulterville, CA.

12. Pope John Paul's recent encyclical, "Veritatis Splendor,"
does not overtly emphasize processing life, but rather emphasizes
forming one's conscience in accord with the moral truth revealed
by the Church. We agree with the need to consider the moral
norms taught by the Church and to have an informed conscience. However, in Matthew 19:16–22, which is the very text
used as the basis for this encyclical, Jesus' response to the rich
young man emphasizes life: "If you wish to enter into life . . ."
Religion cannot be a substitute for processing life or for choosing
whatever leads to life's fullness. Jesus then tells the rich young
man that he is not to kill, steal, commit adultery, lie or dishonor
his parents. Yet, with such laws circumstances must be considered, since there are times to kill in self-defense or steal when we
are starving. All law must be interpreted in light of the higher law
of love that Jesus then quotes: "Love your neighbor as yourself."
The young man replies that he has done all this. Jesus then
invites him to "come and follow me," by giving up his addictive
clinging to wealth. Following Jesus is the ultimate norm for Christians. Like the story of the rich young man, Chapter 9 of this
book also invites us to give up addictions by following Jesus and
asking, "What would Jesus do?"

13. Gershen Kaufman, *Shame: The Power of Caring* (Rochester, VT: Schenkman, 1985).

14. Louis J. Puhl, S.J. (Ed. & Trans.), *The Spiritual Exercises of St. Ignatius* (Chicago: Loyola University Press, 1951), 149.

15. Using James Fowler's scheme of seven stages of faith, spiritual abuse would be whatever prevents us from growing into the next stage of faith to which we are called. In Fowler's scheme, during the last four stages faith evolves from 1) "synthetic-conventional" faith, in which I unquestioningly accept the faith held by my parents and friends, to 2) "individuative-reflective" faith, in which I find my own unique expression of faith, to 3) "conjunctive" faith, in which I integrate my own unique faith with the conflicting beliefs of others, to finally 4) "universalizing" faith, in which I am one with people of all faiths.

The film "Malcolm X" shows this journey from synthetic-conventional faith (in which Malcolm follows his Black Muslim friends in believing that God hates whites and loves blacks), to individuative-reflective faith (in which he challenges the leader's scriptural rationalization of sexual abuse), to conjunctive faith (when he discovers in Mecca his brotherhood with all Moslems, white as well as black).

While I (Sheila) was at the stage of synthetic-conventional faith, it would have been abusive if Christians had pushed me to leave the Jewish faith of my parents and friends. However, when I was at the conjunctive stage, it would have been abusive if my Jewish family had tried to keep me from joining the church by insisting that a Jew could not become a Christian.

Cf. James Fowler, *Stages of Faith: The Psychology of Human Development & the Quest for Meaning* (San Francisco: Harper, 1981) and his updated *Stages of Faith & the Public Church* (San Francisco: Harper, 1991). For how developmental stages (based on the work of Jane Loevinger and Robert Kegan) interact with faith experience in spiritual direction, cf. Elizabeth Liebert, *Changing Life Patterns: Adult Development in Spiritual Direc-*

tion (Mahwah: Paulist Press, 1992). For an integration of faith stages with scripture and family systems theory, cf. Robert T. Sears, S.J., "Healing and Family Spiritual/Emotional Systems," *Journal of Christian Healing*, 5:1 (Spring, 1983), 10–23.

CHAPTER 2: SEXUAL ABUSE & GOD THE MOTHER

1. Cf. Harville Hendrix, *Getting the Love You Want* (New York: Harper & Row, 1988).

2. Cf. Charles Curran, "Catholic Approaches to Sexuality," presentation delivered at Call To Action conference, Chicago, November 7, 1992.

3. A central theme in Alice Miller's work is the consequences of "German discipline." See especially *The Drama of the Gifted Child* (New York: Basic Books, 1983) and *Banished Knowledge* (New York: Doubleday, 1990). See also Hendrix, *op. cit.*, 19ff.

4. We believe that addictions are our best attempt to belong to ourselves, others, God and the universe. Recovery comes when we find a better, more authentic way to belong. Cf. our book *Belonging: Bonds of Healing & Recovery, op. cit.*

5. Some say that by praying to God as "Father," Jesus was saying that we shouldn't pray to God as anything else. If Jesus had meant for us to call God only "Father," then surely those closest to him would have only prayed that way. Yet eleven times the New Testament records prayers by those closest to Jesus, and in none of the prayers is God addressed as "Father." Thus, Jesus was not teaching that we should not call God anything else. Paul Smith, *The Church with Something to Offend Almost Everyone* (Kansas City, 1989), 81.

In calling God "Abba," which really means something like "Daddy," Jesus' point was not that God is masculine (rather than feminine). Rather, Jesus' use of Abba was meant to communicate that God is as intimate as a loving parent (rather than the distant, patriarchal God-image of his day). For an extensive discussion of feminine language and imagery for God, see Sandra Schneiders, *Women and the Word* (Mahwah, NJ: Paulist Press, 1986); Elizabeth Johnson, C.S.J., "The Incomprehensibility of God and the Image of God Male and Female," *Theological Studies*, 45 (1984), 441–465, reprinted in Joann Wolski Conn, *Women's Spirituality* (Mahwah, NJ: Paulist Press, 1986), 243–260; Bernard Cooke, "Non-Patriarchal Salvation," in Conn, *op. cit.*, 274–286.

We might summarize what we are saying with the words of Pope John Paul I, "God is a Father; more than that, God is a mother." (From a talk delivered on September 10, 1978. The complete text may be found under the title "Praying for Peace," in Matthew O'Connell [Ed.], *The Pope Speaks* [Huntington, IN: Sunday Visitor], 23:4, 314.) Pope John Paul II makes a similar point in his encyclical "Rich in Mercy," note #52, when he speaks of the divine mercy of God as having two aspects, described by two Hebrew words, *rahamim* and *hesed*. *Hesed* means God's fidelity, the fatherly love of God, in which God is faithful to his promises because God is faithful to himself. *Rahamim*, which comes from the Hebrew word *rehem*, meaning womb, refers to the motherly love of God, in which God is tenderly near to her children. This motherly womb-love of God is expressed in Isaiah 49:15: "Can a mother forget her infant, or be without tenderness for the child of her womb? Even should she forget you, I will never forget you." In other words, just as God is more father than any father, God is also more mother than any mother.

6. Erik Erikson, "Womanhood and the Inner Space," in *Identity: Youth and Crisis* (New York: W.W. Norton, 1968), 261–294. See also James Nelson, "Male Sexuality and Masculine Spirituality," *SIECUS Report*, 13:4 (March, 1985), 2.

7. Matthew Fox, *Meditations with Meister Eckhart* (Santa Fe: Bear & Co., 1983), 28.

8. For example, Joann Conn observed among her women students that those who " 'don't mind that God is pictured only as

a man or that we aren't allowed to do the same things men do in the Church' " are constricted in their personal development, whereas those who are developing in their identity experience a strain in their relationship with God if their God image does not include femininity. Thus, if a woman does not see a continuity between her developing identity—her nature as a mature woman—and the nature of God, she will either abandon her own deepest identity or abandon (or at least revise) her belief in God. Cf. Joann Wolski Conn, "Restriction and Reconstruction," in *Women's Spirituality*, op. cit., 14–16. See also Ana-Maria Rizzuto, *The Birth of the Living God* (Chicago: Univ. of Chicago Press, 1979).

Men, too, develop more fully when their image of God includes the feminine. Such men are more balanced in their personalities and more spiritually mature, tend to have better relationships with women, and are more committed to social justice. Cf. Andrew Greeley, *The Religious Imagination* (New York: William Sadlier, 1981), 23–29 and 209–213; Dr. Len Sperry, M.D., "From Teddy Bear to God Image: Object Relations Theory and Religious Development," *Psychologists Interested in Religious Issues Newsletter*, 14:2 (Spring, 1989), 5–8.

9. *National Catholic Reporter* (September 21, 1990). A copy of the 700-page report, also known as *The Report of the Winter Commission*, can be purchased by writing to: Dicks & Co., Ltd., P.O. Box 490, St. John's, Newfoundland, Canada A1C 5K6.

10. A. W. Richard Sipe, quoted in *National Catholic Reporter* (September 21, 1990). See also his book *A Secret World: Sexuality and the Search for Celibacy* (New York: Brunner/Mazel, 1990).

For additional resources on child sexual abuse by clergy, contact The Linkup, P.O. Box 1268, Wheeling, IL 60090, (708) 202–0242.

11. We are indebted to Professor of Religious Studies William Shea for the ideas expressed in this section. He goes so far as to

say, "Fear of women, and perhaps hatred of them, may be just what we have to work out of the Catholic system." *Commonweal* (November 7, 1986), 586–590.

INTRODUCTION TO CHAPTERS 3 THROUGH 7: FOUR ROLES

1. We have found the most helpful book on shame to be Gershen Kaufman, *Shame: The Power of Caring, op. cit.* For the relationship between shame and addictions, see also John Bradshaw, *Healing the Shame that Binds You* (Deerfield Beach, FL: Health Communications, 1988) and Patrick Carnes, *Don't Call It Love* (New York: Bantam, 1991). For shame related to codependency and the concept of carried shame, see Pia Mellody with Andrea Wells Miller and Keith Miller, *Facing Codependence* (San Francisco: Harper & Row, 1989).

2. These four roles, derived from Virginia Satir's model of family therapy, were defined by Sharon Wegscheider-Cruse in *Another Chance: Hope and Health for the Alcoholic Family* (Palo Alto: Science & Behavior Books, 1981). Wegscheider-Cruse further developed the roles in *Choicemaking* (Pompano Beach, FL: Health Communications, 1985), where she referred to them as the hero or superkid, the scapegoat or problem child, the lost child, and the mascot or family clown. Others who worked with the four roles, such as Claudia Black, used other terms to describe them. In *It Will Never Happen to Me* (New York: Ballantine Books, 1981), Black calls the hero the responsible child or the overachiever, the scapegoat is the rebel or non-conformist, the lost child is the silent one, the loner or the adjusting child, and the mascot is the distractor or entertainer. For each of the roles we have used a commonly understood term that clearly distinguishes the behavior, e.g., instead of "mascot," we use "distractor" to describe this child's distracting behavior.

3. Dr. Kevin Leman, *The Birth Order Book* (New York: Dell, 1985), 21. The most well-defined pattern is that of the oldest child who is usually the responsible one. For example, 21 out of the 23 first astronauts were the oldest child or an only child.

CHAPTER 3: THE RESPONSIBLE PHARISEE

1. Anthony DeMello, *Taking Flight* (New York: Doubleday, 1988), 104.

2. Sharon Wegscheider-Cruse, quoted in Anne Wilson Schaef, *When Society Becomes an Addict* (New York: Harper & Row, 1987), 30.

3. Not only the New Testament but also the Talmud humorously criticizes the religiously addictive patterns of the Pharisees:

> There are seven kinds of Pharisees: the "what do I get out of it?" Pharisee; the "I look the part" Pharisee; the "oh my poor head" Pharisee, who walks along the street with his head down so as not to see the women and who bangs against the wall; the pestle-Pharisee, who goes about so bent that he looks like a pestle in a mortar; the "what is my duty so that I may do it?" Pharisee; the "I do one good deed every day" Pharisee; and lastly the only real Pharisee, the one who is a Pharisee from fear of God and out of love for Him (Henri Daniel-Rops, *Daily Life in the Time of Jesus* [New York: Hawthorne Books, 1962], 438).

4. *'Pass It On'* (New York: Alcoholics Anonymous World Services, 1984), 384.

5. Responsible children need to receive love in order to care for others in a healthy way. A recent national study of those in the religious life asked them to name which of their peers were "the most caring religious." Then the researchers studied the ones who were named to see how these "caring religious" differed from the other religious. They were the most joyful, related personally

to those they served, and did not burn out. Besides receiving love from others, they were also adept at receiving love from God through contemplative prayer. They were four times more likely to speak of a personal, loving, healing God. To the degree a responsible child receives love, she or he receives the gift of caring in a joyful, life-giving way rather than in a manner that leads to codependency and burnout. Cf. "Motivations Found in Study of Why Helpful Folks Help," *Minneapolis Star Tribune* (October 10, 1992), 10E.

CHAPTER 4: THE REBEL SAMARITAN

1. This is an example of the cycle of abuse. Alice Miller writes, "Any person who abuses his children has himself been traumatized in his childhood in some form or another. This statement applies without exception . . ." Miller, *Banished Knowledge, op. cit.,* 190. See her entire book for how abuse is passed on.

2. *Newsweek*, (May 21, 1990), 76.

3. Addictions may be classified as "attraction addictions" and "aversion addictions." An attraction addiction is the compulsive use of any substance or process in order to escape from our own reality, especially painful feelings. An aversion addiction is the compulsive avoidance of any substance or process in order to escape from our own reality, especially painful feelings. Gerald May gives a list of possible aversion addictions in his book *Addiction & Grace* (San Francisco: Harper & Row, 1988), 38–39.

4. Joachim Jeremias, *Jerusalem in the Time of Jesus* (Philadelphia: Fortress, 1969), 352–358.

5. In fact, the Church does have a long tradition of respect for the exercise of individual conscience vis-à-vis religious authority, although that tradition has not always been emphasized in recent years. For example, in the thirteenth century the canonist Hostiensis wrote,

If the subject cannot bring his conscience into conformity with his prelate's [which implicitly included the pope], then he should follow his conscience and not obey . . . even if his conscience is wrong. (Quoted in Philip Kaufman, *Why You Can Disagree and Remain a Faithful Catholic* [New York: Crossroad, 1989], 151.)

The beloved Cardinal John Henry Newman was an especially great defender of the right of conscience within the Church.

Some Catholic writers dilute freedom of conscience by saying that a person is free to follow his conscience only when it is "properly formed"—meaning, it seems, only when it conforms to the views of religious authority. But Newman's description of what he meant by freedom of conscience is enlightening. Suppose, he said in his *Letter to the Duke of Norfolk*, that the pope ordered all priests in England to give up drink or decreed that there be a lottery held in every English parish.

Suppose, further, that there was a particular priest who liked a little sip of wine after dinner or felt in his heart that gambling was a sin. What was he to do? "That priest in either of these cases would commit a sin," Newman wrote, "if he obeyed the pope, whether he was right or wrong in his opinion." Newman concluded this letter with a delightful observation: "If I am obligated to bring religion into after-dinner toasts (which, indeed, does not seem quite the thing) I shall drink—to the pope, if you please—still, to conscience first, and to the pope afterwards." (Murray J. Elwood, "Newman's 'Kindly Light' Still Brightly Shines," *NCR*, June 1, 1990, 11.)

Pope Pius XII also defended the primacy of individual conscience when he wrote,

Conscience is the innermost and secret nucleus in man. It is there that he takes refuge with his spiritual faculties in absolute silence alone with himself and his God. Conscience is a sanctuary *on the threshold of which all must halt*, even in the case of a child, his father and mother . . ." (Radio Broadcast of March 23, 1952).

The Second Vatican Council continued this tradition of respect for conscience. For example, the document "On Religious Freedom" says, "The Christian faithful, in common with all other men, possess the right not to be hindered in leading their lives in accordance with their conscience" (No. 13).

6. William Sloane Coffin, Jr., "Be Angry But Do Not Sin: A Spirituality for the Long Haul," *Pax Christi*, 14 (1989), 31.

7. *Bread Rising*, 2:8 (December, 1992), 2. As a teenager, Catherine showed early promise as a rebel. She rebelled against her wealthy family by cutting her hair, refusing to marry, staying in her room for 3 1/2 years, and then leaving to work with the poor.

8. Linda's story is told more fully in Dennis & Matthew Linn and Sheila Fabricant, *Praying with Another for Healing* (Mahwah, NJ: Paulist Press, 1984), Chapters 3 and 8. Our prayer with her is recorded in program #3, "Blocks to Healing Prayer," of our video and audio tape series *Praying with Another for Healing* (Mahwah, NJ: Paulist Press, 1984).

CHAPTER 5: THE LOST ESSENE

1. William Saroyan, *Mama I Love You* (Boston: Little Brown, 1956), 154–155.

2. With the current release of photographs of the Dead Sea Scrolls, there seem to be almost as many theories about the Essenes as there are archeologists because, like the lost child, the Essenes concealed well their identity. (Cf. *Minneapolis Star Tribune*, December 23, 1992, 4A.) In our description of the Essenes we rely on the hypothesis of the majority of scholars, that the Qumran community was Essene.

3. David Freedman, *Anchor Bible Dictionary* (New York: Doubleday, 1992), II, 621. Josephus gives an account of the Essenes cult-like behavior, such as starving on grass because they refused to eat the food of non-Essenes.

4. Mary Jane, Dennis & Matthew Linn, *Healing the Dying* (Mahwah, NJ: Paulist Press, 1979).

CHAPTER 6: THE DISTRACTOR SADDUCEE

1. Anthony DeMello, *Taking Flight* (New York: Doubleday, 1988), 18.

2. Erikson divided the human life span into eight developmental stages, each with its own task. We have spoken of how the four roles correspond to the tasks of the four stages of childhood. The four roles also correspond to the tasks of the adolescent and adult stages of life. Adolescents (whose task is identity) need the gift of the rebel in order to form an identity that is separate from their family and culture. Young adults (whose task is intimacy) need the gift of the lost child in order to develop their inner life and become capable of sharing themselves in an intimate relationship with another. Adults in mid-life (whose task is generativity) need the gift of the responsible child in order to care for the next generation. Adults in old age (whose task is integrity) need the distractor's gift of enjoying life (of being rather than doing), in order to face diminishment without succumbing to despair.

CHAPTER 7: GENERATIONAL HEALING OF SPIRITUAL ABUSE

1. Robert Bly, *A Little Book on the Human Shadow* (San Francisco: Harper, 1988), 41.

2. Cf. Dennis Linn, Matthew Linn and Sheila Fabricant Linn, *Healing the Greatest Hurt* (Mahwah: Paulist Press, 1985),

for how we can pray for our ancestors through the communion of saints, including the scriptural and theological basis for generational healing. This book is written from a Roman Catholic perspective, but includes Protestant viewpoints.

3. Stephen Karpman identified the "Rescue Triangle," in which victims, persecutors and rescuers interact and trade places. This dynamic may help us understand how an individual or a group may at times be the lost child victim, the rebel persecutor or the responsible rescuer. We wonder if an addition to Karpman's system might be what we would call the distractor bystander. Karpman's triangle is described in Claude Steiner, *Scripts People Live* (New York: Grove Press, 1974).

4. We first learned about Michael and Julie Weisser and Larry Trapp through an interview with Daniel S. Levy that appeared in the February 17, 1992 issue of *Time* (pages 14 & 16). We recently talked with Michael and Julie, who shared details of their story that were not included in the *Time* interview. Katheryn Watterson is writing a book about the relationship between the Weisser family and Larry Trapp.

INTRODUCTION TO CHAPTERS 8 & 9: WHAT DOES JESUS SAY & WHAT WOULD JESUS DO?

1. Alice Miller, *Banished Knowledge*, *op. cit.*, 33 & 35.

CHAPTER 8: SCRIPTURE & SPIRITUAL ABUSE

1. Anthony DeMello, *The Song of the Bird* (Anand, India: Gujarat Sahitya Prakash, 1982), 57–58.

2. Paul did not challenge the cultural blinders of his time that tolerated slavery because he believed that Jesus was returning soon. Paul expected that everything, including social institutions

such as slavery, would be transformed in the parousia. However, Jesus did not come soon, and the magisterium of the Church proceded to take Paul's toleration of slavery out of context, and interpret Paul's words literally to justify ongoing active support for slavery. For example, in 655, the Ninth Council of Toledo, attempting to enforce recent and much-disputed celibacy laws, declared that the children of married priests would be permanent slaves of the Church. Still trying to enforce celibacy, in 1089 Pope Urban II gave princes the power to enslave the wives of priests. During the Crusades Popes Alexander III and Innocent III authorized the enslavement of captured Christians who had helped the Saracens. In 1454, Pope Nicholas V gave Portuguese explorers permission to "capture, conquer and subjugate all Saracens and pagans whatsoever . . . and to bring their persons into perpetual slavery." In the United States prior to the Civil War, some bishops recommended better treatment for slaves, but none condemned slavery itself as immoral. In 1866, after slavery had been abolished in the United States, the Holy Office continued to affirm the moral justification for slavery, by issuing an instruction that said slavery need not be contrary to the

> natural and divine law, and there can be several just titles of slavery. . . . It is not contrary to the divine law for a slave to be bought, sold, or given, provided that . . . due conditions are observed.

In 1891, in *Rerum novarum*, Pope Leo XIII spoke of the dignity of human labor in such a way that implicitly condemned slavery (no. 44). However, his statement was so muted that it was frequently overlooked and many prominent Roman Catholic moral theologians continued to teach the morality of slavery well into the middle of this century. This Catholic teaching on slavery was not corrected officially until 1965, at Vatican II (*Lumen gentium,* nos. 27 & 29). Even then, the condemnation of slavery was directed at forced labor and slavery in totalitarian countries. The Church did not acknowledge her own history of false teaching and practice of slavery (Kaufman, *op. cit.* 22–24).

As in the above example of how the magisterium interpreted Paul's words in Ephesians 6:5, cultural blinders usually rely upon a literal interpretation of scripture. Down through the centuries interpreting all of scripture literally has led not only to slavery, but to many other abuses, such as the consignment of all Jews to hell at the Council of Florence in 1442, and the imprisonment of Galileo. The scriptural foundation for the inquisition was a literal understanding of "A man who does not live in me is like a withered, rejected branch, picked up to be thrown in the fire and burnt" (Jn 15:6). Another example is Pope Urban VIII, who took literally, as applying to himself, Matthew 28:18: "All authority in heaven and on earth has been given to me." Urban therefore decided that he had personal jurisdiction over every human being. So, he gave half of the globe to Portugal and the other half to Spain.

3. Ann Belford Ulanov, *Receiving Woman* (Philadelphia: Westminster Press, 1981), 134. Based upon an essay by Valerie Saiving Goldstein, "The Human Situation: A Feminine Viewpoint," in Simon Doniger (Ed.), *The Nature of Man in Theological and Psychological Perspective* (New York: Harper & Row, 1962), 151, 153, 165.

4. We are indebted to Michael Crosby, O.F.M. Cap., who first alerted us to the relationship between Matthew 16 and Matthew 18. In his book *The Dysfunctional Church* (Notre Dame: Ave Maria, 1991), Crosby emphasizes that the hierarchical principle of authority (Matthew 16) and the collegial principle of authority (Matthew 18) cannot be divorced from one another. Cf. pages 49–52.

In a more recent interview, Crosby suggests some possible implications of the collegial principle for the celebration of the sacraments:

More and more at reconciliation services I'm saying to people, "You decide if you want to come to me as a representative of Matthew 16 or go to each other as representatives of Matthew 18 because the scripture says the power to bind and loose is in both of them." Catholics are going to have to find new ways to be a church as they find it less tenable to be a church totally controlled by Matthew 16. They have to get over the fear of deciding if these rituals can really be sacraments even without a priest being present. We do need to redefine what sacrament is.

These are rituals instituted by Christ—who is the priest—to give grace. If Catholics don't have a representative of Matthew 16 to break the bread with and if they break bread together and do it in memory of Jesus, *is he going to be present among them?* I believe that is a real form of the presence of God. Isn't this *Real* Presence, too? . . . Catholics don't even know how to celebrate the sacraments in the way I think Jesus intended them because we have become so limited by the clerical expression of the sacrament. (Excerpted from *SALT* [Claretian Publications, June, 1992] in *Bread Rising*, 2:8 [December, 1992], 1.)

5. A vivid contemporary example of returning to an abuser is Anita Hill. During her testimony at the confirmation hearings for Clarence Thomas, she described how she continued to work for him despite his sexual harassment of her. Some who discounted Anita Hill's testimony argued that if her charges were true, surely she would not have continued to work for Thomas. Although we cannot prove who was telling the truth during the confirmation hearings, we do know that the behavior Anita Hill described in herself is typical of persons who are sexually abused or harassed by authority figures. We regret that experts on abuse were not brought into the hearings to explain this aspect of victim psychology.

6. Our Roman Catholic tradition and many other Christian traditions share two beliefs about afterlife. The first belief is that heaven exists and people are there. (By "heaven" we don't mean a

literal place, but rather a state of loving union.) We all have loved ones—grandparents, parents, friends—who we are confident are in heaven. Secondly, hell exists as a possibility, but we don't know if anyone is there. (By "hell," we mean a state of supreme alienation.) If anyone is in hell, it is not because God sent that person there, but because he or she chose it. C.S. Lewis used the image of hell as a room with the door closed from the inside, our side. But "neither Jesus, nor the Church after him, ever stated that persons go there or are actually there now" (Richard McBrien, *Catholicism* [Study Edition] [Minneapolis: Winston, 1981], 1152). We know only that we are not to judge, and we are to pray that all of us open our hearts to God.

For a more extensive discussion of whether God vengefully punishes and the problem of hell, see John Sachs, "Current Eschatology: Universal Salvation and the Problem of Hell," *Theological Studies*, 52 (1991), 227–254.

7. For a more complete discussion of this passage, see Kenneth Bailey, *Poet & Peasant and Through Peasant Eyes* (Grand Rapids, MI: Eerdmans, 1980), 1–21 ("The Parable of the Two Debtors").

8. The concept of an "enlightened witness" in the healing of abuse comes from Alice Miller. See her book *Banished Knowledge, op. cit.*

9. Loretta Jankowski, Presentation to Conference on "Women: Oneness of Being & of Spirit," Boise, ID, February 9, 1991.

10. Cf. James Lockman, O.F.M., "Re-examining the Parable of the Pounds" (unpublished paper, Graduate Theological Union, Berkeley, CA).

11. The problem with proof-texting is that the Bible contains not only historical and scientific errors, but also moral errors. For example, Joshua 11:14–15 speaks of the total destruction of a group of people considered as the enemy, and justifies this as the will of Yahweh. Today we regard this as morally unacceptable and we call it genocide. Although the Bible does not contain in

every passage scientific, historical or moral truth, it does always contain "salvific truth." Thus all of scripture must be read in light of the overarching message of salvific truth:

> . . . the revelation of God's intention to save all human beings and all that that statement implies. God has promised salvation to humanity, and God is true to that promise.

Cf. Eugene LaVerdiere, "Fundamentalism and the Bible," 15 (unpublished paper presented at the Diocesan Liaisons' Theological Symposium in Plymouth, Michigan, September, 1987), cited in Theodore E. Dobson, *Catholic and Fundamentalist Approaches to the Bible* (Lakewood, CO: Easter Publications, 1988), 13.

About the Authors

DENNIS, SHEILA AND MATT LINN work together as a team, integrating physical, emotional and spiritual wholeness, having worked as hospital chaplains, therapists and currently in leading retreats and spiritual direction. As a team they have taught courses on healing in over thirty countries and in many universities, including a course for doctors accredited by the American Medical Association. Matt and Dennis are the authors of twelve books, the last seven co-authored with Sheila. Their books include *Healing of Memories, Healing Life's Hurts, Deliverance Prayer, Healing the Dying* (with Sr. Mary Jane Linn), *To Heal as Jesus Healed* (with Barbara Shlemon). *Prayer Course for Healing Life's Hurts, Praying with Another for Healing, Healing the Greatest Hurt, Healing the Eight Stages of Life, Belonging: Bonds of Healing and Recovery,* and *Good Goats: Healing Our Image of God.* These books have sold over a million copies in English and have been translated into fifteen different languages.